Minnesota

Minnesota

Martin Hintz

Children's Press®
A Division of Grolier Publishing
New York   London   Hong Kong   Sydney
Danbury, Connecticut

Frontispiece: Early morning on a winter day in Stillwater

Front cover: Third Avenue Bridge, Minneapolis

Back cover: Sunrise near Afton

Consultant: Dallas R. Lindgren, Minnesota Historical Society

Please note: All statistics are as up-to-date as possible at the time of publication.

Visit Children's Press on the Internet at http://publishing.grolier.com

Book production by Editorial Directions, Inc.

Library of Congress Cataloging-in-Publication Data

Hintz, Martin.
    Minnesota / by Martin Hintz.
       144 p. 24 cm. — (America the beautiful. Second series)
    Includes bibliographical references and index.
    Summary: Describes the geography, plants, animals, history, economy, language,
      religions, culture, sports, art, and people of the state of Minnesota.
    ISBN 0-516-21040-8
    1. Minnesota—Juvenile literature. [1. Minnesota.] I. Title. II. Series.
F606.3.H54 2000
977.6—dc21
                                            98-50074
                                                CIP
                                                AC

Acknowledgments

The author wishes to thank the many Minnesotans who proudly showed off their state, including Tom Crain, Dave Bergman, Linda Robinson, Kate Brady, Sheila Gebhard, Dan Collins, Thomas F. Walters, Craig Charles, Denny St. Clair, Barbara Averill, Scott Pengelly, Brian Dietz, Jean Freidl, and Laura McCarthy. Special thanks to Father James Whalen, who got all this writing business up and going many long years ago.

Burntside Lake

Cross-country skiing

A Minnesota farm

Contents

Green Giant statue

Central Avenue Bridge

St. Paul skyline

Minnesota Children's Museum

Randall Cunningham

CHAPTER ONE

What's in a Name?

Minnesota's lakes are sprinkled across a rolling landscape. In the far north, the lakes are surrounded by thick pine forests. In the south, the lakes extend into fields of farmland. Viewed from above, there seems to be a lake each mile. It is no wonder this state is nicknamed the Land of 10,000 Lakes.

For the record, however, Minnesota has more than 15,000 lakes. Of these, 11,842 cover more than 10 acres (4 hectares). Try naming that many lakes! It is easy to start running out of possibilities. That's probably why there are 156 Long Lakes, 83 Bass Lakes, and at least 3 Swan Lakes.

Minnesotan mapmakers chose descriptive names such as One-Mile Lake, Two-Mile Lake, Round Lake, and Twin Lake. They used the names of various animals: Bear, Buffalo, Leech, Eagle, Cormorant, Heron, Loon, and Perch. They also named lakes after plants and trees: Rice, Walnut, Beech, and Black Oak. American Indian names were popular too: Minnewaska, Osakis, Esquagamah, and Wabedo. Some lakes were named for ethnic groups: German and Scotch. Others were named after people:

Charlotte, Martin, Trenton, Harriet, Florence, Dora, Rickert, and Saint Olaf. Some names for Minnesota's lakes are even more creative: Diddle de Woodle, Woman, Echo, Ripple, Dismal Swamp, Bologna, Little Boy, and Deer Yard.

Why does Minnesota have so many lakes? Ten thousand years ago, the region was caught in the tight grip of the Ice Age. When the towering glaciers melted, crystal-clear lakes were created. The shoreline of all these lakes adds up to more than that of Hawaii, California, and Florida combined.

With all these available bodies of water, it is not surprising that there is one boat registered for every six Minnesotans and every town seems to have a fishing tournament. Of course, the state is proud of its extensive calendar of water shows, the largest of which is the Minneapolis Aquatennial in July.

Minnesota's northeastern system of lakes and rivers along the Boundary Waters Canoe Area shares the border with Canada. Up north, a tip of Minnesota around Lake of the Woods contains the Northwest Angle State Forest and part of the Red Lake Indian Reservation. This tip, which looks like the squiggle of a mapmaker's pen, is actually the northernmost point of the United States, not including Alaska.

Looking for a Nickname

In the early days of Minnesota Territory, the settlers argued about what nickname to give their region. For a time, it was called the Beaver State because large numbers of these valuable fur-bearing animals lived along Minnesota's streams and rivers.

In 1859, an opportunity for a new name came along. At the

time, an attempt was being made to amend the state constitution. Some lawmakers wanted to allow the state to issue $5 million in bonds to help railroads add more track. In 1857, opponents of the amendment had published a cartoon showing ten men weighed down with bags of money, supposedly representing ten legislators bribed to pass the act. On their backs was a railroad track carrying a line of train cars pulled by nine gophers. Other gophers in the cartoon were singing and telling puns with the names of amendment supporters. The drawing quickly became known as the "Gopher Cartoon," and Minnesota was soon tagged the Gopher State, after the striped, burrowing rodent.

As a footnote, the railroad bond bill eventually passed. But the

Lake of the Woods is on the border of Minnesota and Canada.

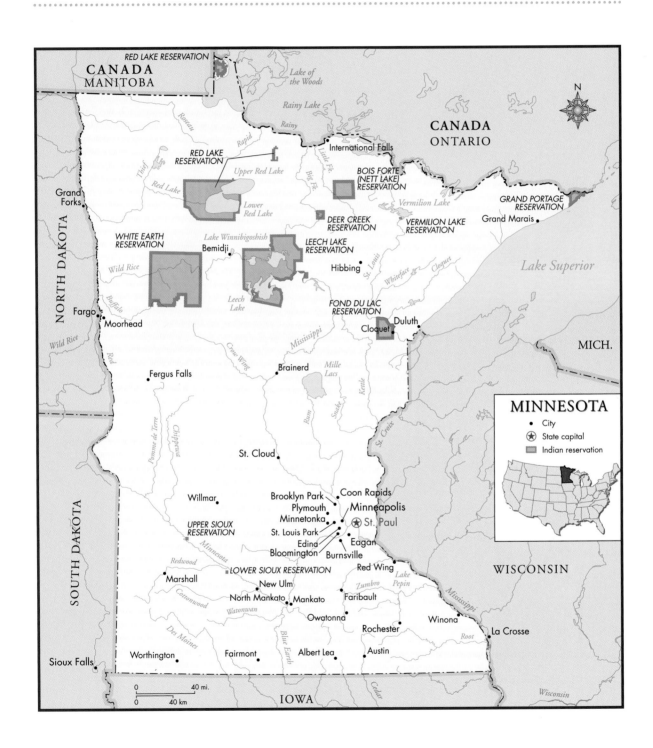

RED LAKE RESERVATION

CANADA
MANITOBA

Lake of
the Woods

Rainy Lake

CANADA
ONTARIO

N

Roseau

Rapid

Rainy

International Falls

RED LAKE
RESERVATION

Little Fk.

BOIS FORTE
(NETT LAKE)
RESERVATION

GRAND PORTAGE
RESERVATION

Grand
Forks

Thief

Upper Red Lake

Big Fk.

Red Lake

DEER CREEK
RESERVATION

Vermilion Lake

VERMILION LAKE
RESERVATION

Grand Marais

Lower
Red Lake

NORTH DAKOTA

WHITE EARTH
RESERVATION

Lake Winnibigoshish

Bemidji

LEECH LAKE
RESERVATION

Hibbing

St. Louis

Lake Superior

Wild Rice

Whiteface

Cloquet

Fargo

Buffalo

Leech
Lake

FOND DU LAC
RESERVATION

MICH.

Moorhead

Cloquet

Duluth

Wild Rice

Red

Crow Wing

Mississippi

Mille
Lacs

Brainerd

Fergus Falls

Kettle

Pomme de Terre

Chippewa

Rum

Snake

St. Croix

St. Cloud

MINNESOTA

• City

⊛ State capital

▨ Indian reservation

SOUTH DAKOTA

Willmar

Brooklyn Park   Coon Rapids

Plymouth

Minneapolis

Minnetonka

⊛ St. Paul

St. Louis Park

UPPER SIOUX
RESERVATION

Edina

Eagan

Minnesota

Bloomington   Burnsville

Redwood

LOWER SIOUX RESERVATION

Red Wing

Lake
Pepin

WISCONSIN

Marshall

New Ulm

Zumbro

Cottonwood

North Mankato   Mankato

Faribault

Mississippi

Watonwan

Owatonna

Winona

La Crosse

Des Moines

Blue Earth

Rochester

Root

Sioux Falls

Worthington

Fairmont

Albert Lea

Austin

Cedar

Wisconsin

0   40 mi.

0   40 km

IOWA

railroads couldn't complete their work in time and the state was saddled with a debt that took more than twenty years to pay off. It was a heavy financial burden, exactly as the cartoon predicted.

Whether Minnesota is called the Gopher State, the Land of 10,000 Lakes, or the North Star State (the state's official nickname), there is never a slow moment in Minnesota. In the rugged winters, Minnesotans ice skate, cross-country ski, and race dogsleds. During the rest of the year, hikers climb the Tettegouche State Park trails, sports enthusiasts attend Minnesota Twins and Vikings games, and children ride the Ferris wheel at the Minnesota State Fair. Fans of *The Wizard of Oz* visit the Judy Garland Museum in Grand Rapids, and those wishing for a little quiet sit in the tall Indian grass at Maplewood State Park, just as Laura did in Laura Ingalls Wilder's popular book *Little House on the Prairie*.

Opposite: Geopolitical map of Minnesota

Cross-country skiing, a favorite winter activity

CHAPTER TWO

The First Minnesotans

Lake of the Woods, on the border between Minnesota and Canada, was the perfect setting for a small group of Native Americans. Their ancestors were fur-clad hunters—Paleo-Indians. They probably came from Asia and crossed the Bering Sea to North America over a land bridge that linked the continents thousands of years ago.

Early inhabitants of Minnesota hunted the mastodon.

In the quiet wilderness, the hunters walked along the rocky shore. They fished the lake's waters and stalked large elephantlike animals called mastodons in the nearby forest. In the late afternoon, they camped by the water, huddling under their furs. When ice crusted over the back bays, the hunters moved inland.

The next frosty morning, the band moved on, leaving behind some broken spear points and other household debris. Thousands of years later, those flint artifacts would teach archaeologists something about Minnesota's past.

Earliest Minnesotans

Between 5000 B.C. and 1000 B.C., Eastern Archaic people of the Copper Culture, who are believed to have descended from the Paleo-Indians, wandered along the northern reaches of Minnesota.

Opposite: A buffalo skull and smoking materials at Pipestone National Monument

Early Artwork and Religious Sites in Minnesota

Five thousand years ago, early Minnesotans made carvings and drawings of people and animals on rock faces and the sides of cliffs. Jeffers Petroglyphs in southwestern Minnesota has many excellent examples of their handiwork (left).

Other ancient Minnesotans built intricately shaped mounds for grave sites and religious purposes. An estimated 10,000 of these mounds were scattered around southern Minnesota before the arrival of the white settlers, who often plowed them under. The largest is Grand Mound near International Falls. ■

These early Minnesotans created weapons and tools from copper, a valuable metal found throughout the Upper Great Lakes region. Copper was easy to smelt and make into harpoons, fishhooks, and other items.

Eventually, the Copper Culture faded and was replaced by the Northeast Woodland Culture. The forests of northern Minnesota were the perfect habitat for these skilled woods dwellers and they enjoyed a comfortable lifestyle. They fished for sturgeon, pike, and whitefish; hunted elk, moose, and deer; and gathered wild rice and berries. They lived in Minnesota from 1000 B.C. to A.D. 1600.

By the early 1600s, the Dakota, or Sioux, and the Ojibwa, or Chippewa, were already spreading throughout Minnesota. Four major groups of Dakota people lived in central and northern Minnesota. They included the Mdewakanton, the Wahpekute, the Sisseton, and the Wahpeton. To the west near the Missouri River were distant relatives of the Dakota. The Yanktons, the Tetons, the Cutheads, and other clans roamed the vast prairies on horseback.

Living in portable tepees, the Dakota and their cousins could pack up and move quickly, usually following the buffalo.

The Ojibwa, longtime enemies of the Dakota, lived primarily along Lake Superior in what is now the Duluth area, which they called Head of the Lake. The Ojibwa had a scornful name for the Dakota—*Natowessiw*, which meant "enemy" or "snakelike ones." The French fur traders translated the Ojibwa word as *Nadouessioux*, which was later shortened to "Sioux."

The Ojibwa, who sometimes called themselves the *Anishinabe* or "the original people," migrated from the eastern shores of Lake

Native Americans lived along the lakes in Minnesota.

French-Canadian fur trappers were drawn to the thick Minnesota woods.

Superior to Minnesota. Their snug, weather-tight homes were clustered in permanent villages. The Ojibwa were excellent traders, traveling throughout the Great Lakes in long birch-bark canoes. However, when they eventually ran into the Dakota who lived inland, fighting erupted over hunting grounds.

Minnesota's First Europeans

When the Europeans arrived, Minnesota was rich in furs, which attracted French-Canadian trappers and traders. Hardy woodsmen called voyageurs paddled down the rivers and trekked through the thick forests. They carried huge packs of goods for trading and returned laden with fur pelts.

The first white people known to reach Minnesota were Pierre Radisson and Médard Chouart, Sieur des Groseilliers. The two explorers traveled throughout the Minnesota wilderness in 1654

A Well-Traveled Priest

Father Louis Hennepin was born in Belgium in 1640. He came to North America in 1675 and began ministering to the Iroquois in Ontario, Canada. In 1678, he traveled through Lakes Erie, Huron, and Michigan and found the upper Illinois River, eventually reaching the site of what is now Peoria, Illinois.

In 1680, the Dakota took the priest captive. Instead of fearing for his life, Hennepin gained an appreciation for the Native Americans' ability to adapt to the demands of their environment. In his journals, he wrote that the Dakota even gave him relaxing steam baths, which must have seemed like a luxury after his long, arduous travels.

After his return to Europe, Father Hennepin wrote numerous stories about his adventures in North America. He died in Rome in 1701. ▪

and 1660. Another early arrival was Nicolas Perrot, who built a fort on Lake Pepin. His tiny outpost was one of the first European settlements in Minnesota.

Frenchman Daniel Greysolon, Sieur du Lhut, roamed northeastern Minnesota between 1679 and 1689. One of his outposts eventually grew to be the city of Duluth. He worked hard to bring peace between the Dakota and Ojibwa nations and convinced them both to sign a treaty in 1679 recognizing the authority of King Louis XIV of France.

Other explorers of the era included Michel Accault and Father Louis Hennepin, a priest who canoed the upper Mississippi River. He was captured by the Dakota in 1680 and rescued by Daniel Greysolon. Many streets, avenues, and parks in Minnesota are named after this explorer-priest.

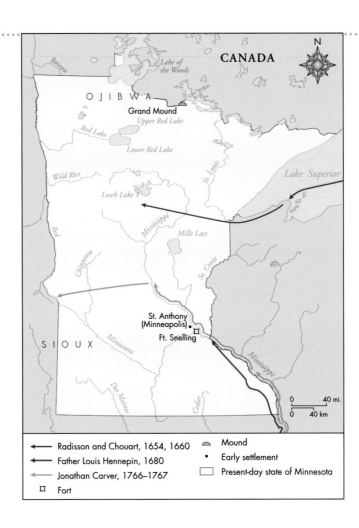

In 1695, Pierre Le Sueur built a fort on Blue Earth River.
Already, Minnesota was experiencing change.

Wars and Territory

Political events in faraway Europe affected even the most remote
frontier settlements during the Seven Years' War, or the French and
Indian War (1756–1763). When the fighting drew to a bloody
close in 1763, victorious England claimed all the French territories

in North America. This included northern and eastern Minnesota, along with all of Canada.

Explorer Jonathan Carver, born in 1710 in Weymouth, Massachusetts, traveled widely around Minnesota in 1766 and 1767. He wrote extensively about his trips, and his interesting tales attracted the attention of many prospective settlers. Carver was followed by David Thompson, a geographer and explorer who recorded the region's topography.

In 1783, the Treaty of Paris, which ended the Revolutionary War, gave eastern Minnesota to the newly formed United States. However, the fledgling country was too weak to protect its frontier. So the English-owned North West Company and Hudson's Bay Company continued to do business in Minnesota until the end of the War of 1812. After the U.S. victory in that conflict, the English companies were finally forced out, and John Jacob Astor's American Fur Company had free rein.

The Louisiana Purchase in 1803 turned western Minnesota over to the United States. Lieutenant Zebulon Pike was ordered to find suitable places to construct forts. In 1805, he made a treaty with the Dakota, and in 1819, Pike took control of the junction of the Minnesota and Mississippi Rivers, where Fort Snelling was eventually established.

Lieutenant Zebulon Pike

Catching the Wild Horse, from George Catlin's *North American Indian Portfolio,* 1844

A Growth Spurt

Under the protection of the U.S. government and its soldiers, Minnesota grew rapidly. Steamboats bringing goods and settlers chugged their way up the Mississippi. More land exploration took place. In 1836, artist George Catlin traveled to American Indian rock quarries, now Pipestone National Monument. His paintings vividly depict the lifestyle and clothing of the Plains Indians he met on his journeys.

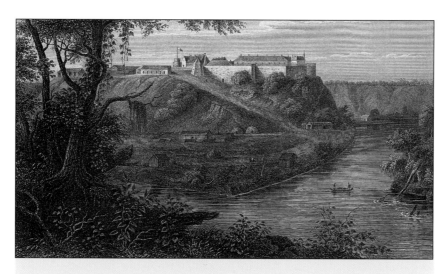

The First Commander of Fort St. Anthony

Colonel Josiah Snelling was the first commander of Fort St. Anthony (above) from 1820 to 1827. The fort was renamed Fort Snelling in 1825. He was a tough and fair-minded officer, but like many military men of the day, he enjoyed drinking. When he drank too much, he had a terrible temper and the fringe of red hair on his balding head would fluff up. The look reminded his men of a ruffed grouse, so they nicknamed him the "Prairie Chicken." ■

Treaties with the American Indians opened up more of Minnesota for white settlement. Subsequently, the Dakota and most Ojibwa were forced to leave their ancestral lands.

In the early 1800s, the boundaries of Minnesota were often changed as the United States juggled the administration of the area. Political control usually depended on whether the land was east or west of the Mississippi River. Parts of Minnesota had belonged to the territories of Illinois, Indiana, Iowa, Mississippi, Missouri, and Wisconsin and the territory and district of Louisiana.

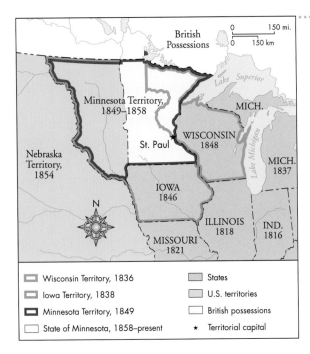

British Possessions

Minnesota Territory, 1849–1858

St. Paul

Lake Superior

MICH.

WISCONSIN 1848

Lake Michigan

MICH. 1837

Nebraska Territory, 1854

IOWA 1846

ILLINOIS 1818

IND. 1816

MISSOURI 1821

N

0   150 mi.
0   150 km

Wisconsin Territory, 1836
Iowa Territory, 1838
Minnesota Territory, 1849
State of Minnesota, 1858–present

States
U.S. territories
British possessions
★ Territorial capital

Historical map of Minnesota

Alexander Ramsey was Minnesota's first territorial governor.

Eastern Minnesota was initially part of Northwest Territory. The region was part of Wisconsin Territory from 1836 until 1848, when Wisconsin became a state with the St. Croix River as its western boundary. This subsequently left land between the St. Croix and Mississippi Rivers without any government at all.

By 1848, the population in Minnesota was large enough to allow the region to become officially Minnesota Territory. Many prominent settlers met in Stillwater that July to discuss the future. They agreed to have their capital in St. Paul, establish a prison in Stillwater, and set up a university in St. Anthony, which later became Minneapolis. On March 3, 1849, Congress passed an act recognizing Minnesota Territory. Business-man Alexander Ramsey, originally from Pennsylvania, was the first territorial governor. The first territorial legislature met on September 3, 1849, and immediately created eight counties and recommended making a territorial seal.

The First Official Use of *Minnesota*

The passage of the act establishing Minnesota Territory in 1849 was the first time the name *Minnesota* was officially used. The word comes from the Dakota words for water—*minne*—and cloudy or sky-tinted—*sotah*. ■

The Dakota Fight for Their Land

While the white settlers worked toward territorial status and eventual statehood, their continued settlement of Minnesota caused conflict with the region's American Indians. In 1857, under the leadership of Inkpaduta, a small band of Dakota known as the Wahpekute attacked settlements in northwest Iowa and southwest

Minnesota. Four women were captured, two of whom were murdered. Other Dakota attempted to seize Inkpaduta's band and successfully bargained for the release of the two remaining hostages.

Although the Dakota brought peace back to the prairies, many of the Indians who pursued Inkpaduta staged an assault a short time

Steps to Statehood

April 30, 1803	Western Minnesota is granted to the United States after the Louisiana Purchase.
March 26, 1804	Minnesota is included in Louisiana Territory.
June 4, 1812	Minnesota becomes part of Missouri Territory.
June 28, 1818	Eastern Minnesota is attached to Michigan Territory.
June 28, 1834	Western Minnesota is attached to Michigan Territory.
April 26, 1836	Eastern Minnesota becomes part of Wisconsin Territory.
July 3, 1836	Western Minnesota is taken into Wisconsin Territory.
June 12, 1838	Minnesota land west of the Mississippi River is given to Iowa Territory.
March 3, 1849	The U.S. federal government recognizes Minnesota Territory.
September 3, 1849	The first territorial legislature meets.
1851	Land west of the Mississippi River is given up by the Sioux.
July 1857	Constitutional convention meets.
May 11, 1858	Minnesota becomes the thirty-second state.

Minnesota's First Newspaper

The state's first newspaper was the *Minnesota Register*, which claimed that it was first printed in St. Paul on April 27, 1849. However, the newspaper was actually printed on a press in Cincinnati, Ohio, two weeks earlier than the date on the masthead because the Ohio-based printer could not ship the equipment upriver to Minnesota because of floods. Still, the *Register's* first issue came out a day earlier than that of the *Pioneer*, which was actually printed in the territory. The *Pioneer* was the forerunner of today's *St. Paul Pioneer Press*.

later. In 1862, they attacked an Indian agency and fort after promised government payments for their land failed to arrive.

By 1857, Minnesota Territory had a population of 150,037, large enough to apply for statehood. In July 1857, a convention drew up Minnesota's first constitution, which was adopted the following October. On May 11, 1858, Minnesota became the Union's thirty-second state.

CHAPTER THREE

The Dawning of a New Age

The new state of Minnesota was ripe for development. Eager immigrants, mostly from Europe, poured in. Norwegians, Swedes, and Germans headed west to the wide-open prairies, hungrily looking for land to farm. Irish, Ukrainians, and Slovaks were also represented. Some newcomers got there on foot, while some came on horseback and others hitched rides on freight wagons or traveled by stagecoach or steamboat.

Immigrants saw that Minnesota offered plentiful land to farm and mine.

A Landmark Slavery Decision

In the late 1850s and early 1860s, Minnesotans were caught up in discussions about slavery, an issue that was soon to tear the United States apart. The state was the backdrop for a historical controversy involving a slave named Dred Scott.

Dred Scott and his future wife, Harriett, were brought to Fort Snelling by their owners. In 1836, Dred and Harriett were married, and Harriett's owner sold her to Dred's owner, Dr. John Emerson. At the time, Fort Snelling was in free territory—slavery was not allowed. The law was not always followed on the frontier, however, and no one officially objected to the Scotts' bondage. When Emerson returned to live in the slave state of Missouri, he took the couple with him.

Opposite: Minneapolis in the 1880s

Dred Scott and his wife were the subjects of a famous Supreme Court case about slavery.

After Emerson's death, the Scotts sued his widow in court, arguing that they should be considered free because they had been taken to live in free territory. The U.S. Supreme Court did not agree. In 1857, the Court decided that Scott had no right to sue because no black—free or slave—could become a U.S. citizen. It also said that Congress had never had the authority to ban slavery.

The *Dred Scott v. Sandford* decision, which made slavery legal in all the territories, bolstered a strong anti-slavery movement in Minnesota. State residents began hiding escaped slaves. One outspoken opponent of slavery was Jane Grey Swisshelm, owner of a St. Cloud newspaper that was often attacked for its anti-slavery position. She was also one of the first organizers for the Republican Party in Minnesota and worked to elect Abraham Lincoln as president.

A Drover Named Joe Rolette

In the 1850s, carts were used to haul freight along the remote Red River frontier with Canada. The wide-wheeled carts made of wood, rawhide, and canvas were light enough to traverse wet ground but sturdy enough to carry huge loads. Drawn by oxen, the carts traveled about 15 miles (24 km) a day. At night, the drovers arranged their carts in a circle and slept inside the protective ring.

Each drover was usually responsible for four carts that traveled in single file. The oxen in each team were tied to the cart in front of them. The drovers, usually of mixed Indian and white descent, were a tough, colorful bunch who often wore wide sashes around their waists. A portrait of drover Joe (Jolly Joe) Rolette hangs in the Minnesota capitol. He was also one of Minnesota Territory's first legislators.

Rolette objected to a bill that had been passed to move the territorial capital from St. Paul to the town of St. Peter, so he played a trick on his fellow lawmakers. He hid the official copy of the legislation and holed up for more than a week with his old drover buddies, playing poker and drinking whiskey. When it was too late for the bill to be signed, Rolette reappeared, saving the day for St. Paul. ■

Civil War Breaks Out

War was in the air as the United States entered the 1860s. The Southern states felt that the Northern states were threatening their way of life, economically and politically. They felt that states' rights were more important than the national government. They eventually seceded, or broke away, from the Union and set up their own government called the Confederate States of America.

When the American Civil War began in 1861, Minnesota troops were the first to volunteer to fight for the Union. Many of them assembled at Fort Snelling. During the war, almost 25,000 Minnesotans enlisted and thousands died—in battle or from disease. They served with distinction throughout the war, earning particular praise for their courage at the Battle of Gettysburg in far-off Pennsylvania.

Bloodshed in Minnesota

Although Minnesota was far from the Civil War's front lines, the state saw its share of bloodshed. The Dakota people's frustration with the white settlers and the U.S. government deepened. Without their hunting grounds or the promised payments from the government, Dakota families often went hungry. They were now crowded into a strip of land only 10 miles (16 kilometers) wide on the south side of the Minnesota River.

When the young Dakota warriors watched troops leaving the state to fight in the South, they saw an opportunity to drive out the white settlers once and for all. Fighting broke out in August 1862, and the Western frontier was again in flames. Death toll estimates of settlers and soldiers range from 400 to almost 1,000. An unknown number of Dakota were killed, including the respected warrior Little Crow, who had objected to the fighting but felt obliged to support his people.

Refugees poured into Blue Earth, hiding behind hastily dug fortifications. New Ulm was attacked and burned. Thousands of settlers fled to eastern Minnesota. Merton Eastlick was only eleven years old when the Dakota attacked his family's farm near Lake Shetek. Most of his family and many neighbors were killed in what became known as Slaughter Slough. But Merton hid in the weeds and eventually carried his younger brother Johnny more than 50 miles (80 km) on his back to safety.

After a few weeks of bloody fighting between the Dakota and U.S. troops, led by Colonel Henry H. Sibley, the terror faded. Thirty-eight Dakota men were hanged for their alleged role in the war. The conflict left twenty-three southwestern counties virtually unpopulated, but it wasn't long before the settlers returned.

Life on the Prairie

It was not easy living on the prairies. Settlers had to contend with swarms of locusts, drought, floods, snowstorms, and never-ending hours of work and loneliness. The children were lucky if a one-room school was nearby. Their parents banded together in groups such as the Grange, also called the Patrons of Husbandry. They not only made friends in these organizations but also lobbied for better prices for their crops and worked hard to ensure that their interests were represented in the state legislature.

As a youngster, author Laura Ingalls Wilder (1867–1957) lived in Walnut Grove in Minnesota's farm belt. One of her books, *Little House on the Prairie*, was made into a successful, long-running television show in the 1970s. Near her hometown is the McCone Sod House, a replica of the sod

Laura Ingalls Wilder at age seventeen

House, a replica of the sod homes that many early settlers lived in. The earthen house was snug but probably hard to keep clean!

Railroads to the West

The railroads were a driving force in opening up the prairies. In 1857, the U.S. Congress had contributed a huge grant of land to Minnesota Territory to encourage railroad construction. The terri-

Bringing Pioneer History Alive

Several sites near the Twin Cities of Minneapolis and St. Paul bring history alive for young visitors. Shakopee's historic Murphy's Landing (right) has artifacts and displays dating from the 1840s through the 1890s. Costumed guides describe frontier life and show visitors around. Minnesota Pioneer Park in Annandale is a tribute to the hardy folk who carved their farms out of the state's Big Woods, a vast stretch of oak, pine, and maple trees. The park includes a homesteader's house, farm stables and sheds, a Soo Line Depot, a one-room schoolhouse, and other structures from pioneer days. ■

The Northern Pacific Railroad at its crossing in Brainerd, 1871

James J. Hill, known as the Empire Builder

tory was authorized to sell parcels of this land to railroad companies that promised to lay tracks.

Construction on the state's first railroad, the Minnesota & Pacific Railroad, began in 1862 to link St. Paul with St. Anthony, which would become Minneapolis. It was the initial leg of a line that became known as the Great Northern Railway, the tracks of which eventually stretched from St. Paul to the Pacific Ocean. James J. Hill, nicknamed the Empire Builder because he was one of the most powerful men in Minnesota, owned the company. His enormous house stands across the street from the Roman Catholic Cathedral on the bluffs above downtown St. Paul.

By the 1870s, up to 104 trains daily carried many new immigrants into the spacious St. Paul Union Depot. Thousands of Poles and Finns went on to the mines and lumber camps in the far north, Germans and Swedes headed for the rich farming country, and others remained in the crowded capital city.

Industry and Mechanization

By the mid-1800s, Minnesota was well into the Industrial Age. Large industry evolved from the first small lumber mills that sprang up along the Mississippi River. At the time, the federal government estimated that there were at least 10 billion board feet (24 million cubic meters) of white pine lumber in Minnesota. In the 1890s, mills in Minneapolis were turning out almost 470 million board feet (1.13 million cu m) of prime lumber a year. A large quantity of quality lumber was produced in those busy days.

Logging was big business in Minnesota during the late 1800s.

Minneapolis also quickly became the leading flour producer in the world, using grain from the prairie farms. In 1881, the Pillsbury Company opened the world's largest flour mill there, turning out tons of thick white flour every day.

Near the mills were coopers, or barrel makers, tanneries, and ironworks, and jobs were plentiful. In September 1882, electricity helped light up these factories. It was the first time in the United

Outlaw Jesse James Comes to Minnesota

Northfield, Minnesota, earned a place in history when Jesse James and his outlaw gang raided the town bank on September 7, 1876. A clerk and several gang members were killed in the holdup.

Each autumn, the town re-creates the holdup during its Jesse James Days Festival. Bullet holes from the attack can still be seen in some of the town buildings. ■

The Founding of Maternity Hospital

In 1887, Dr. Martha Ripley founded Maternity Hospital (above) in Minneapolis. In the 1800s, most women gave birth to their babies at home. As few hospitals admitted women who were unmarried or without homes, Dr. Ripley's hospital filled an important need and received widespread attention for its quality of care. An ardent feminist, Dr. Ripley supported the rights of women to vote and laws protecting the family and women from violence. ■

States that electricity generated by water power was delivered to factories through wires.

Mechanization changed the lives of all Minnesotans. By the turn of the century, about a dozen automobiles were in use around the state. In 1902, one man had already been arrested for exceeding the state's 10-mile (16-km)-per-hour speed limit. By 1910, Minnesotans owned more than 7,000 automobiles and 4,000 motorcycles.

The advent of the gasoline engine also benefited Minnesota farms. The first gasoline tractors chugged across the fields in 1910. At first, farmers laughed at the newfangled contraptions, saying that nothing pulled a plow as well as a horse or mule. Eventually, however, they appreciated the advances in technology, including the Minnesota Agricultural Extension Service's advice about increasing their crop yields with fertilizers and pesticides. Some wanted to turn their farms into "food factories" that operated much like industrial plants.

Minnesota was one of the first states to tax gasoline to pay for new roads and the first to number its highways, a system that the other states eventually followed. And if machines were already on the ground, why not in the skies? The first airplane flew over Minneapolis in 1913. It was the dawning of a new age for Minnesota.

Minnesota farms became more productive after the turn of the century.

CHAPTER FOUR

Changing Times

n the early twentieth century, things in Minnesota were changing rapidly. With so many men serving in World War I (1914–1918), women went to work in industrial plants, wearing overalls and carrying lunch buckets. They worked in factories around the state, including Minneapolis Steel and Machinery Company. After the war, some women found it hard to go back to being housewives. When American women won the right to vote in 1920, the United States had to rethink its traditional ways.

Business continued its postwar boom, and almost everyone was making money on the stock market, at least on paper. In 1920, alcohol was outlawed in the Eighteenth Amendment to the U.S. Constitution. Rules of enforcement were highlighted in the National Prohibition Act, or Volstead Act, named after Congressman Andrew Volstead of Minnesota. Restrictions on drinking went into effect on January 17, 1920, but the law was regularly broken.

Gangsters soon moved in to supply the demand for illegal alcohol, and St. Paul became a haven for criminals. City police and crooks had an unwritten truce: the gangs promised not do their dirty work in the city and the cops left them alone. Ma Barker and Baby Face Nelson were among the mobsters who found a quiet haven in St. Paul between their violent excursions outside the city.

The National Prohibition Act was also known as the Volstead Act, after Congressman Andrew Volstead.

Opposite: Women working in a Minnesota factory during World War I

Despite the smuggled booze and upbeat music and dancing, trouble loomed. The lumber industry in the northern woods was dying out. Many farmers had borrowed too much money for more land and new equipment. Investors thought the good times would last forever. When the harsh reality of the Great Depression hit Minnesota in the 1930s, many people lost everything. The depres-

The 1934 truck drivers' strike resulted in a riot.

sion was a worldwide financial crisis, and it affected even the most remote Minnesota homesteads.

About 70 percent of the Iron Range miners were out of work. In the Twin Cities of St. Paul and Minneapolis, long lines of desperate men and women looking for jobs formed outside factories. Unable to pay the mortgages on their homes, many families were forced to live in makeshift shanties along the Mississippi River. People wrote to Governor Floyd Olson asking for help, but he was powerless. During a 1934 strike, police and truck drivers battled in the streets of Minneapolis, and several workers were killed. At least some were satisfied when Prohibition, an admitted failure, was repealed in 1933.

It seemed as though the world was caving in. One bright spot was President Franklin D. Roosevelt's New Deal programs. A federal program called the Civilian Conservation Corps helped thousands of Minnesotans, putting young people to work on public projects. They built bridges, roads, parks, and campgrounds that are still in use, making Minnesota a national leader in outdoor recreation facilities. Even Native Americans benefited from the New Deal programs. Through Roosevelt's efforts, the United States began a long, slow crawl back to economic recovery.

World at War Again

War clouds again swept over the world when Germany attacked its neighbors in the late 1930s, starting World War II (1939–1945). America entered the war after Japan bombed U.S. military installations in Pearl Harbor, Hawaii, on December 7, 1941. Soon Minnesota's iron mines and industrial plants expanded to produce guns, ammunition, and uniforms. More than 300,000 Minnesotans joined the armed forces, and 6,000 died serving their country.

On the home front from Cannon Falls to Cloquet, women returned to the factories. Children planted so-called Victory Gardens of vegetables in their backyards so that commercially grown food could be sent to the troops. Hollywood Caravans, traveling

Republican Harold Stassen

When he was elected governor at age thirty-one in 1938, Harold Stassen was the youngest Minnesotan ever to serve in that position. The popular Republican was reelected twice. During World War II, he left office to join the U.S. Navy. In 1945, Stassen helped draft the charter for the United Nations.

In the early 1950s, Stassen became an adviser to President Dwight D. Eisenhower. Among his many duties, he directed the program that gave foreign aid to war-torn Europe. Many thought he would make an excellent president, but his Republican colleagues never nominated him. Stassen continued his work for peace and became an authority on disarmament. ■

shows with movie stars such as Cary Grant and Olivia de Havilland, visited Minneapolis and St. Paul to raise money for the war effort.

The war ground to a bloody halt in 1945, and thousands of young men and women returned to Minnesota, eager to meet new challenges. Many veterans took advantage of the GI Bill, a federal financial-aid package for higher education. To accommodate the flood of veterans returning to school, long metal huts were constructed on the campuses of the University of Minnesota and the College of St. Thomas in St. Paul, among others, for use as classrooms and dorms. The crowding paid off when the highly educated veterans entered the civilian workforce.

Postwar Attitudes

After the horrors of World War I, many Minnesotans had became isolationists—people who supported a national policy of avoiding political and economic relations with the rest of the world. However, after World War II, they felt a responsibility to stay involved in international affairs. In 1945, when the U.S. Senate voted to join the United Nations, the once popular senator Henrik Shipstead of Minnesota was one of only two senators to oppose the measure. Out of step with the times, he lost his next election by a landslide. In 1946, most Minnesotans realized that their country had an important role to play on the international front.

Economic Growth and Preservation Pressures

The 1950s were strong years for Minnesota economically. The old boundaries between rural and city life faded fast. The use of

Minneapolis in the 1950s

machinery increased as young people left agriculture for life in the cities. Over the next thirty years, the farm population dropped to less than 5 percent of all state residents. In the meantime, sprawling suburbs gobbled up rich farmlands and important wetlands. The state's Department of Natural Resources and environmentalists struggled with industries and land developers to find a middle ground between growth and preservation.

There were successes and setbacks for both sides. In 1957, the state created a planning commission for the Twin Cities area in response to the exploding populations of Minneapolis, St. Paul, and neighboring communities. In 1967, the commission was given new authority as the Metropolitan Council to help coordinate governmental functions ranging from park management to snow removal. By the 1990s, some 60 percent of Minnesota's residents lived in an urban strip between the Twin Cities and St. Cloud.

Other population centers grew across state lines. Duluth, Minnesota, linked with Superior, Wisconsin. Fargo, North Dakota, became a sister city to Moorhead, Minnesota. La Crosse, Wisconsin, just across the Mississippi River, was a major employment draw for thousands of Minnesotans.

Postwar Mining Industry

After World War II, the state's mining industry also grew. Minnesota's large mines—closed when their high-quality ore was depleted—were later opened to excavate taconite, a lesser grade of iron ore. The completion of the St. Lawrence Seaway in 1959 meant that the port of Duluth could accommodate the huge freighters needed to haul Minnesota ore to mills in the eastern United States or to processing plants overseas. However, state taxes on taconite hindered the growth of the mining industry.

In 1964, Minnesotans approved a constitutional amendment that boosted investment in the mining industry by declaring that taxes on taconite could no longer be set at a higher rate than taxes on other natural resources. In the past, the difference had discouraged ore producers from mining and processing taconite. After passage of the amendment, valid for twenty-five years, the mine owners pumped more than $1 billion into their industry.

Water, Land, and Air Transportation Growth

In this fast-paced time, construction for transportation was increasing. Twenty-seven dams were built on the Mississippi River between 1930 and 1963. Locks at each dam could raise or lower water to allow freight-hauling barges to move to the next level. The docks in the Twin Cities, Red Wing, and other port cities were busy again.

Freeways linked Minnesota with the rest of the United States. By 1979, a motorist could drive all the way from Minneapolis to New York without stopping at a single red traffic light.

The Twin Cities international airport was expanded and became the hub for Northwest Airlines. The company, formed in 1926 as Northwest Orient Airlines, is the fourth-largest U.S. air carrier. The rest of the world was now only hours away from Minnesota. In the 1990s, Northwest Airlines had more than 2,600 daily flights from almost 250 airports around the world.

U.S. senator Eugene McCarthy opposed the Vietnam War.

Postwar Politics and Beyond

The Democratic-Farmer-Labor (DFL) Party won its first major election in the 1954 governor's race. The streetwise Orville Freeman, who became secretary of agriculture under President John F. Kennedy in the 1960s, headed the party's ticket of candidates. Minnesota's behind-the-scenes campaign strategists such as Eugenie Moore Anderson earned national attention for their political smarts.

In the 1960s, Minnesotans were confronted with serious social issues ranging from civil rights to the Vietnam War. Senator

Eugene McCarthy became a spokesman for antiwar groups and made a strong bid for the Democratic presidential nomination. However, at the party's riotous convention in Chicago in 1968, delegates chose another Minnesotan to head their ticket—Vice President Hubert H. Humphrey. McCarthy's supporters on the streets outside lost to the representatives inside the convention hall who backed the former Minneapolis mayor and longtime U.S. senator.

Hubert Humphrey speaking in New York City

Minnesotan Walter Mondale was vice president under President Jimmy Carter.

During the late 1960s, the University of Minnesota was a hotbed of antiwar fever as students protested the Vietnam War. Many young Minnesota men slipped easily across the border to Canada to evade being drafted to fight in the unpopular conflict.

In 1968 in Minnesota, the American Indian Movement (AIM) began to attract frustrated young people from various Indian nations. AIM leaders led the Trail of Broken Treaties march to Washington, D.C., in 1972 to call attention to problems on the reservations. In 1973, Minnesota Indians were among those who took over Wounded Knee, a small town in South Dakota, to protest government treatment of Native Americans. During the ensuing seventy-one-day siege, two people were killed and several were wounded. In a widely publicized trial in St. Paul, the AIM leaders were acquitted and released.

Other Minnesotans made their mark on the national scene as the 1960s blended into the next decades. In 1969, St. Paul's Warren Burger was appointed chief justice of the U.S. Supreme Court. Another Minnesotan, Harry Blackmun, was named to the Supreme Court in 1970. In 1976, Walter Mondale was elected vice president under Democratic president Jimmy Carter.

In 1984, Mondale launched his own presidential campaign with Geraldine Ferraro—the first woman vice-presidential nominee. Although they campaigned hard, Mondale and Ferraro were defeated by Ronald Reagan and his team in a landslide. Mondale later served as ambassador to Japan.

With the state's growth, however, came responsibilities and challenges. While Minnesota benefited from having the taconite plants up and running, the industry was polluting the water and air. In 1978, the Minnesota Supreme Court ordered the Reserve Mining Company of Silver Bay to improve their pollution control. In 1980, the firm built a waste-disposal site and stopped dumping contaminated water into Lake Superior. It was only one of many efforts to find a balance between economic progress and environmental health.

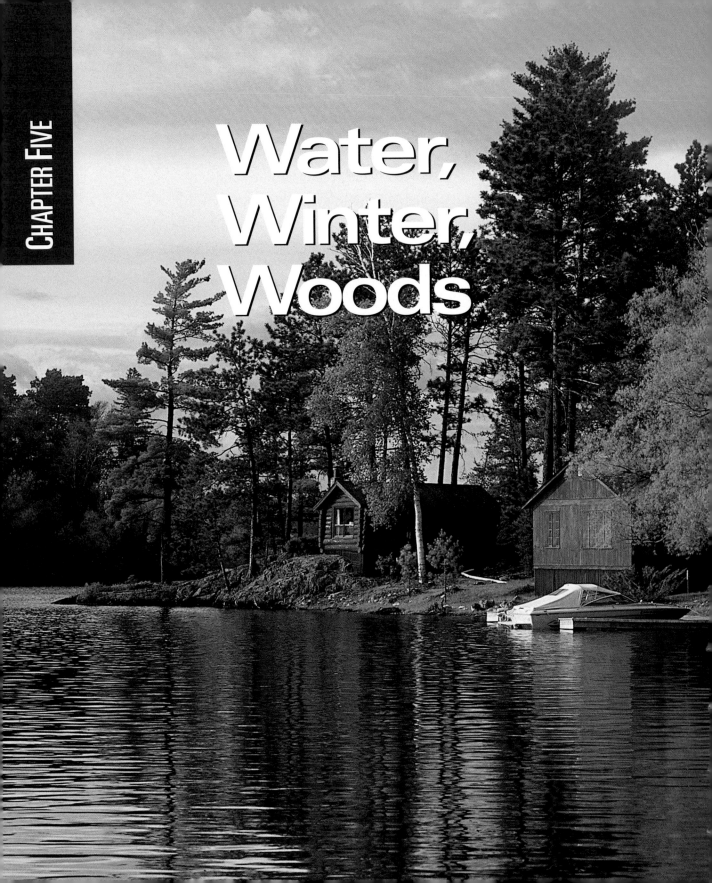

CHAPTER FIVE

Water, Winter, Woods

Minnesota's farms rely on the state's fertile soil.

During the Pleistocene epoch 2 million years ago, hundreds of feet of ice, inching slowly southward from Canada, buried Minnesota. The last glaciers began to retreat only 20,000 years ago.

These heavy sheets of snow and ice carried rocks and gravel with them. The weight of the ice and the rocks helped to level out the land underneath. Only a small part of southeastern Minnesota called the Driftless Area was spared. In this region, steep bluffs and high ridges still rise over the land. Elsewhere, the land is gently rolling or relatively flat, with rich, fertile soil that was beneficial to the early pioneers. All the low places filled with water from the melting ice pack and became lakes and marshes.

Minnesota's greatest north-south distance is 407 miles (655 km) and its greatest east-west distance is 360 miles (580 km). It is bounded by Canada on the north, Lake Superior and the Mississippi and St. Croix Rivers on the east, North and South Dakota on

Opposite: Cabins at Burntside Lake, near Ely

the west, and Iowa on the south. The entire state encompasses 86,943 square miles (225,182 square kilometers).

Beyond the state's geography, Minnesota's northern and southern regions have their own philosophies and outlooks on life. The pristine wooded lake region north of the Twin Cities is prime vacationland studded with campgrounds, resorts, and summer homes. Southern Minnesota, with its bustling cities and productive farms, has a different pace.

The Boundary Waters Canoe Area

The Superior Uplands

The Superior Uplands region, one of four major land regions in Minnesota, is an extensive stretch of hard rock that the glaciers did not affect much. The state's highest point, Eagle Mountain in Cook County, rises above the green treeline to 2,301 feet (702 meters). This mineral-rich tip of Minnesota is called the Arrowhead region after its shape.

Voyageurs National Park and the Boundary Waters Canoe Area lie along the Canadian border between International Falls and Lake Superior. Here, canoeists often spot eagles diving for fish, and deer and moose drinking at the shoreline. In this place, people "carry-in, carry-out" their garbage in an effort to leave nothing of the modern world behind.

Autumn colors at Superior National Forest

The Split Rock Light-house is a state historic site.

Directly east of Voyageurs National Park is the Superior National Forest, which covers most of the Arrowhead region. The Chippewa National Forest in north-central Minnesota also offers plenty of outdoor recreation.

Palisade Head is at the far end of the Arrowhead. This granite outcropping rises 300 feet (92 m) above the chilly waters of Lake Superior. From a lookout point, it is easy to see the Apostle Islands and the Wisconsin shoreline on the far southern horizon. Split Rock Lighthouse, a state historic site, stands nearby. The lighthouse was completed in 1910 to warn freighters of the dangerous rocks around the shore.

The Young Drift Plains

The Young Drift Plains region, in central and western Minnesota, the state's second distinct landform, is made up of low, rolling farmlands. Glaciers did a fine remodeling job on the landscape here, practically rolling the ground flat. "Drift" refers to the thick topsoil left behind after the ice melted—some of the best farmland in the United States. The area's few hills are also the result of the glaciers. They are moraines, or ridges of leftover rock, dumped in long, snakelike lines that once marked the perimeter of retreating ice.

The northernmost point of the Drift Plains around the Canadian border is the bed of prehistoric Lake Agassiz. Its waters were once greater than all of today's Great Lakes combined, covering what is now the Red River Valley and extending far north beyond Lake Winnipeg. Because ice blocked the northern end, the glacial melt had to run south. The torrent cut a valley more than 1 mile (1.6 km) wide and up to 200 feet (61 m) deep. The lake drained away thousands of years ago, leaving farmland, marshes, and woodlands. The former lakebed is so flat that some early farmers claimed that they could plow a straight line for 7 miles (11 km).

Sand hills, now covered with vegetation, once formed the beaches for the ancient lake and can be seen along the eastern edge of the Red River Valley. State Highway 11 roughly follows the rim of what was once Lake Agassiz. American Indians, fur traders, and trappers took the same route generations ago. Some of these ancient beaches are now more than 40 miles (64 km) from the closest water.

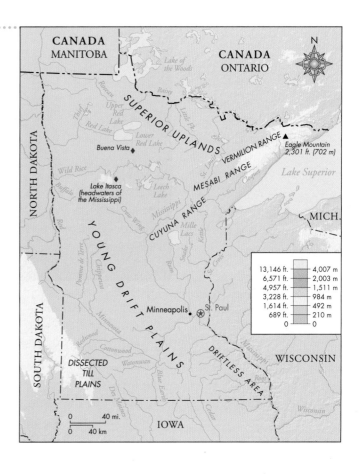

Minnesota's topography

The Dissected Till Plains

The Dissected Till Plains region, the third major land type in Minnesota, covers the southwestern corner of the state. "Dissected" means that small streams and rivers cut through the land, forming gullies and shallow valleys. "Till" is a mixture of sand, clay, pebble, and gravel that is usually good for farming.

Grand Portage National Monument

To travel Minnesota's lakes, it is often necessary to carry, or portage, canoes and gear from one lake to the next. It is amazing to think that the old-time French-Canadian voyageurs carried up to three packs of raw hides, weighing 100 pounds (45 kg) each, plus all their gear, through the thick tangle of woods.

The reconstructed trading post of Grand Portage (above) is now a national monument. It marks the end of the 8.5-mile (13.7-km) trek that the traders had to portage to get around the rough rapids of the Pigeon River. ■

The Driftless Area

The rock-ribbed Driftless Area, Minnesota's fourth land feature, is tucked into the far southeast corner of the state. This hilly region borders Iowa and the Mississippi River, which fattens out into Lake Pepin in one area. Numerous, fast-moving trout streams and the Cannon and Root Rivers meander along the base of high, flat-topped ridges. This was how all of Minnesota probably looked before the Ice Age.

The Northwest Angle Way Up North

The Northwest Angle is a chunk of the state of Minnesota that lies on the Canadian side of Lake of the Woods. In the 1783 Treaty of Paris, due to an imperfect land survey, the area was made part of the United States instead of Canada. As a result, this small portion of Minnesota rock and pine is accessible from the United States only by water. The village of Penasse there receives most of its income from tourism and logging. The Northwest Angle measures about 130 square miles (337 sq km). ■

Minnesota's Geographical Features

Total area; rank	86,943 sq. mi. (225,182 sq km); 12th
Land; rank	79,617 sq. mi. (206,208 sq km); 14th
Water; rank	7,326 sq. mi. (18,974 sq km); 4th
Inland water; rank	4,780 sq. mi. (12,380 sq km); 3rd
Great Lakes water; rank	2,546 sq. mi. (6,594 sq km); 5th
Geographic center	Crow Wing, 10 miles (16 km) southwest of Brainerd
Highest point	Eagle Mountain, 2,301 feet (702 m)
Lowest point	Lake Superior, 602 feet (184 m)
Largest city	Minneapolis
Population; rank	4,387,029 (1990 census); 20th
Record high temperature	114°F (46°C) at Beardsley on July 29, 1917, and at Moorhead on July 6, 1936
Record low temperature	–60°F (–51°C) at Tower on February 2, 1996
Average July temperature	70°F (21°C)
Average January temperature	8°F (–13°C)
Average annual precipitation	26 inches (66 cm)

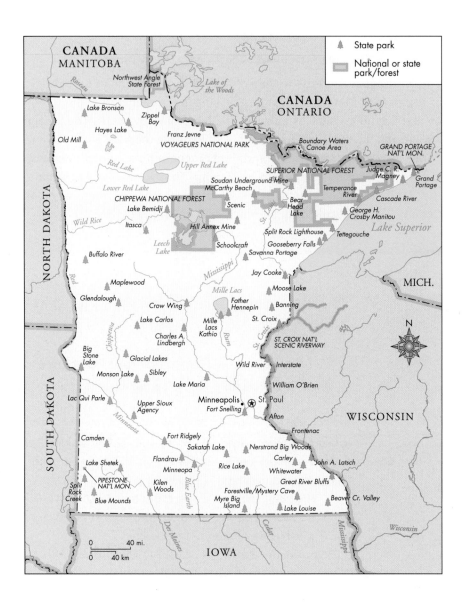

Minnesota's parks and forests

Guides at the Forest Resource Center outside Lanesboro take kids into the bluff country to learn about the plants, animals, and geography of the limestone-rich region. Nearby Mystery Cave at Forestville features four species of bats and spooky crystal shapes.

Lakes and Waterfalls

Minnesota has one of the greatest expanses of water of any U.S. state. The state has an estimated 15,000 to 22,000 bodies of water large enough to be considered lakes. In addition to these lakes, 2,546 square miles (6,594 sq km) of Lake Superior, one of the Great Lakes, is under Minnesota's management. Northern Minnesota's Red Lake is the state's largest lake, covering 430 square miles (1,114 sq km).

Lake Superior is partially managed by Minnesota.

Tourists at the head-waters of the Mississippi flowing into Lake Itasca

Lake Itasca is one of Minnesota's most important lakes. It is sometimes called the headwaters for the Mississippi River, which flows out of the lake as a narrow stream only about 10 feet (3 m) wide and less than 2 feet (61 cm) deep. However, the Mississippi's actual headwaters are the many streams that flow into Lake Itasca from higher elevations.

Up to 57 percent of Minnesota is drained by the Mississippi River and its tributaries. The river's major branches are Crow Wing, Minnesota, St. Croix, Sauk, and Rum Rivers. The Rainy and Red Rivers drain the northern and northwestern parts of the state. The St. Louis empties into Lake Superior.

The Founding and Legends of Lake Itasca

Henry Rowe Schoolcraft (right) found Lake Itasca in 1832. Not that it was ever lost, of course, because the American Indians always knew of its existence. He coined the word *Itasca* from the Latin words *veritas* and *caput*, which mean "truth" and "head" because it was the "true head" of the Mississippi.

According to Ojibwa legend, the lake was named in honor of I-tesk-a, the daughter of Hiawatha, the American Indian folk hero. The legend says that she was carried away by the lord of the underworld because of her beauty, and her tears formed the Mississippi. Another tale about the lake's creation involves another folk hero, Paul Bunyan, and Babe, his giant blue ox. It is said that Babe accidentally tipped over a water tank in a logging camp, which created both the lake and the river. ■

Minnehaha Falls after a snowfall

Numerous waterfalls occur along these rivers. One of the prettiest is Minnehaha Falls on Minnehaha Creek in Minneapolis. These falls, which drop 53 feet (16 m), were made famous by poet Henry Wadsworth Longfellow in his *Song of Hiawatha*. The St. Anthony Falls are 16 feet (5 m) high. The state's highest waterfall is the 124-foot (38-m) Cascade Falls on the Cascade River in Cook County. Canada and Minnesota share the Pigeon River's 133-foot (41-m) High Falls.

A Climate of Contrasts

Winter visitors to Minnesota may be surprised to discover that the state has a moderate climate. Minnesotans take a certain pride when national weather watchers report the frigid winter temperatures that sometimes occur in Minnesota. When the winter winds blow, the town of International Falls often records particularly low temperatures. The low of −59° Fahrenheit (−51° Celsius) at Pokegama Dam on February 16, 1903, was the state record until February 2, 1996, when the temperature dropped to −60°F (−51°C) in the village of Tower. However, the average winter temperature is about 8°F (−13°C), at least in January.

A summer picnic in Northfield

Summers are pleasant, with an average July temperature of around 70°F (21°C). The state's highest recorded temperature was 114°F (46°C) at Beardsley on July 29, 1917, and again at Moorhead on July 6, 1936. Summer mosquitoes thrive in Minnesota's warm weather; occasionally they are called "the state birds" because of their size and number.

Southeastern Minnesota has the state's highest precipitation, receiving 32 inches (81 centimeters) a year. About 19 inches (48 cm) of rain and snow fall on northwestern Minnesota a year. To the delight of snowmobilers and skiers, snowfall averages 20 inches (51 cm) in the southwest and 70 inches (178 cm) in the northeast. In the thick northern forests, snow may remain on the ground until early May.

Birch trees in Superior National Forest

Forests and Wildlife

Woods cover some 35 percent of Minnesota's land. Spruce, birch, pine, balsam fir, and aspen, along with the beautiful shrubs sweet fern, cranberry, honeysuckle, and dwarf kalmia, carpet the north. Black walnut, elm, maple, ash, and oak, along with sumac, ironwood, and thorn apple, thrive in the south.

Cattails, arrowhead lilies, and asters grow in the swamps.

Minnesota has an estimated 7,500 plant species, including wild roses, lilies of the valley, and wild geraniums. The largest wildflower in Minnesota is the water lily.

One of the largest caribou herds in the United States roams the 445,500-acre (180,428-ha) Beltrami Island State Forest in northern Minnesota. The forest's peat bogs are full of blueberries, a favorite snack for black bears. Weasels, bats, woodchucks, rabbits, lynx squirrels, moose, deer, and gophers abound. Several packs of wolves now live in the state.

Wildflowers brighten the fields of Minnesota.

The weasel and many other animals inhabit the Minnesota forests.

Minnesota's birds include quail, pheasants, blue jays, crows, sparrows, robins, and various duck species The state is on the Mississippi flyway, the annual route for tens of thousands of migrating fowl. Anglers cast in the bountiful lakes and rivers for perch, bass, trout, walleye, catfish, and sturgeon.

With sixty-eight state parks and fifty-seven state forests, Minnesota provides many opportunities to learn about the environment. The state's Department of Natural Resources sponsors a MinnAqua education program to teach residents about lake and stream ecology. Project Learning Tree is another state-sponsored environmental education program that teaches youngsters about Minnesota's land, air, and water.

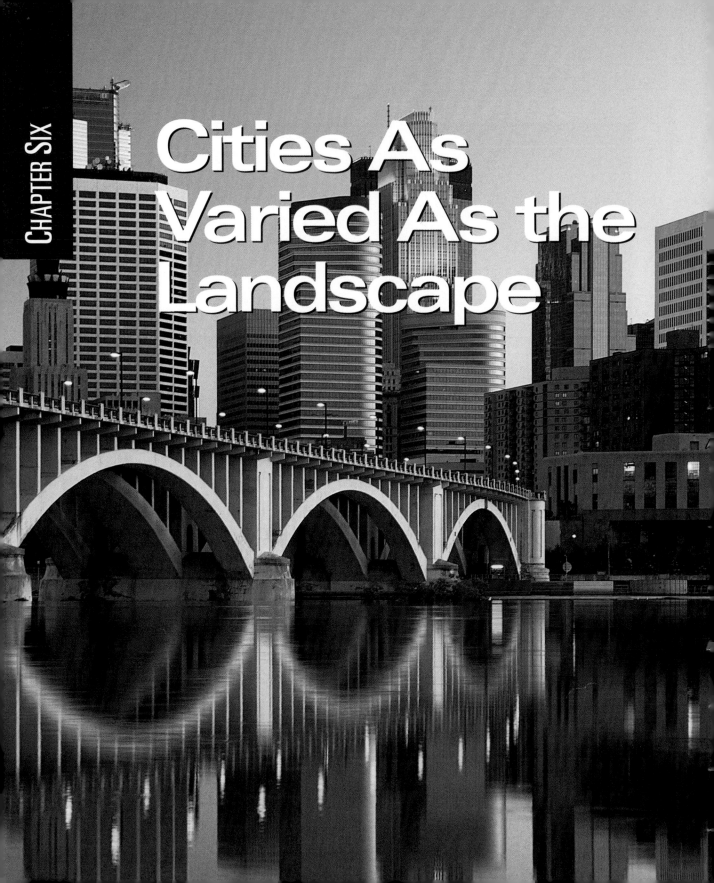

CHAPTER SIX

Cities As Varied As the Landscape

M innesota is a vibrant mix of small-town friendliness and urban bustle. Although forests or farmland often come to mind when people think of Minnesota, more of its residents live in towns and cities than in the country.

A brief tour of Minnesota's communities begins in the state's southwest corner. Blue Earth got its name from its blue-tinged clay. Peas and beans flourish here, making the town a perfect home for the Green Giant packing plant. During the June-through-July harvest, Blue Earth is crowded with trucks carrying fresh produce. Green Giant hires hundreds of part-time workers to process the vegetables and get them to market quickly.

The town of Pipestone lies west of Blue Earth. Many of its buildings are made of a hard red rock called Sioux quartzite that is quarried from nearby pits. But Pipestone is better known for—and named after—a softer, mottled-pink stone. The Dakota believe that the rock is the color of their ancestors' blood. Today, only Native Americans are permitted to extract pipestone from the quarries in Pipestone National Monument. Skilled craftworkers chisel the soft rock into intricate pipes, jewelry, and statuettes. Their handiwork is on display in the Upper Midwest Indian Cultural Center on the monument grounds.

Urban bustle of St. Paul

Opposite: Central Avenue Bridge, Minneapolis

Summer prairie grass at Pipestone National Monument

Far north of Pipestone is Viking. The state's far northwestern corner, from the northern border with Canada to the western borders with North and South Dakota, is sometimes called Vikingland after the thousands of immigrants from Sweden and Norway who settled here in the late 1800s. Some believe that Scandinavian Vikings made their way to the prairies centuries earlier. A stone supposedly carved with Scandinavian lettering, or runes, that tells of an exploration through the region was found in a farm field near Alexandria. Most historians, however, consider the stone a fake.

The Heritage Hjemkomst Interpretive Center in Moorhead pays tribute to the region's Scandinavian past by housing a replica of a Viking longship, 77 feet (23 m) long. High school counselor Robert Asp built the vessel, but he died in 1980 before he could sail

A Giant Who Eats His Vegetables

The now-familiar "Green Giant" was introduced by the Minnesota Valley Canning Company in 1925 as a bearskin-wearing figure promoting a new variety of peas. In 1929, he reappeared as a vegetable-eating giant in a suit of leaves. In 1950, the company changed its name to Green Giant.

Although the cannery has been through various changes over the years, the "Jolly Green Giant" still stands tall in Blue Earth. A statue of the giant (right)—55.5-foot (17-m) high and weighing 8,000 pounds (3,600 kg)—can be seen from the freeway in Blue Earth. This Green Giant wears size 78 shoes and, in the winter, a red scarf around his neck. The statue was dedicated on July 6, 1979, to mark the last completed Interstate 90 link between the East and West Coasts. ■

the ship to Norway. In 1982, a crew sailed the vessel 6,100 miles (9,815 km) from Duluth, Minnesota, to Bergen, Norway.

In the center of Minnesota is the village of Lake Itasca, home to the headwaters of the Mississippi River and Itasca State Park, which covers 32,000 acres (12,960 ha). Here you can step across the mighty Mississippi as it begins its 2,340-mile (3,765-km) journey from Lake Itasca to the Gulf of Mexico. But be careful—slipping on the rocks and wetting your feet is considered bad luck.

North of Lake Itasca is Bemidji, which gets its name from an Ojibwa word meaning "lake with river flowing through." The town is the heart of Minnesota's northern country, where folktales about Paul Bunyan and Babe, his huge blue ox, abound. According to these fanciful stories, the two were the greatest logging team in the towering white pine forests. Bunyan chopped the timber and Babe pulled the logs to the mills. Tall statues of Bunyan and his bovine

Racing Turtles

Throughout the summer, the International Turtle Races are held in Perham, a resort town in west-central Minnesota. The first turtle to cross outside a circle drawn on the ground wins the race. Anyone can enter a turtle. ■

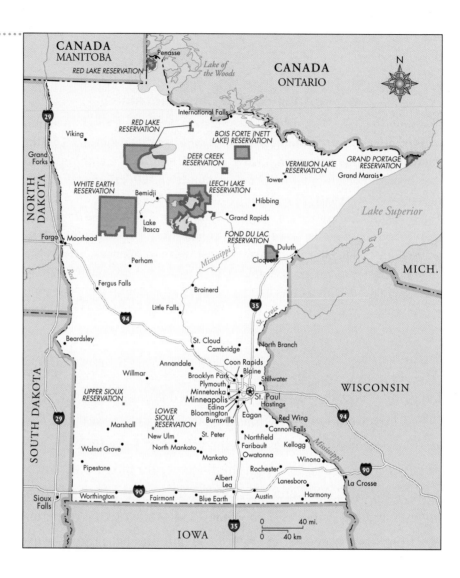

Minnesota's cities and interstates

buddy are major tourist attractions in town. In Bemidji, it is not officially spring until both are scrubbed clean.

South of Lake Itasca is Little Falls, named after the Mississippi River rapids that powered the town's famous sawmills and flour mills. The city is also the boyhood home of Charles A. Lindbergh Jr., a famous pilot. Papermaking and boat-building are the city's main industries.

On the eastern state border, Duluth is Minnesota's fourth-largest city, with more than 85,000 residents. The city has long been a major Lake Superior commercial hub. More than 40 million tons of cargo a year pass through its port. Crossing the harbor entrance is a 386-foot (118-m) aerial-lift bridge linking the mainland with a spit of sand and rock called Minnesota Point. The Point is a favorite location for summer homes, from which residents can watch the passing ships. The Canal Park boardwalk is a perfect place to watch the lake freighters.

Minnesota's largest communities are in the east-central section. According to the 1990 census, Minneapolis–St. Paul had more than 600,000 residents.

Because the Mississippi River snakes between the two cities, Minneapolis has been called "the first city of the West" and St. Paul, the state capital, "the last city in the East." The waterway wig-

The Lone Eagle Flies Across Atlantic

In 1927, Charles A. Lindbergh Jr. flew the first solo nonstop flight across the Atlantic from New York to Paris. His small plane was called the *Spirit of St. Louis*. As the result of his daring trip, he became a national hero, earning nicknames such as Lucky Lindy and Lone Eagle. Lindbergh's boyhood home in Little Falls is now a museum in the heart of Charles A. Lindbergh State Park. ■

Along the waterfront trail at Duluth

Fort Snelling—A Living Museum

In 1819, Fort Snelling was built at the point where the Mississippi and Minnesota Rivers meet. The fort served as an active duty site through World War II. Barracks, a chapel, a hospital, a store, and other buildings have been reconstructed and the facility is now a living museum. Guides dressed as soldiers and their families tell about life on the frontier. There are blacksmith demonstrations, firings of muskets and cannons, and parades. A view from the ramparts showcases the impressive Twin Cities skyline. ■

The St. Paul skyline as seen from Indian Mounds Park

gles around so much that some parts of each city are on opposite banks, which can be very confusing. The University of Minnesota campus straddles the river with a covered bridge.

Minneapolis is the larger of the Twin Cities. With its office towers and business pace, it is considered more cosmopolitan than St. Paul, which appears to have a calmer, quieter air. St. Paul's hills are crowned by the domes of the state capitol and the Roman Catholic Cathedral of St. Paul.

People often forget that St. Paul was originally called Pig's Eye Landing, after an early fur trader and settler named Pierre (Pig's Eye) Parrant. In 1841, French priest Lucien Galtier built a small log church near Parrant's Landing and named it in honor of Saint Paul. Father Galtier suggested that the growing village around the church use the name and the city agreed. Incorporated in 1854, the city of St. Paul remained the capital when Minnesota became a state in 1858.

Residents of each city share the Twin Cities' theaters, art galleries, sports complexes, and parkland. For instance, the Minneapolis Institute of Arts and the Walker Art Center are in Minneapolis, while the Ordway Music Center and the Fitzgerald Theater are in St. Paul. The Steppingstone Theater features young performers from around the Twin Cities.

Bloomington, a suburb of Minneapolis, is the state's third-largest city. While it is the home of the sprawling, multileveled Mall of America, the solitude of the Minnesota Valley National Wildlife Refuge Center is only a few blocks away.

The rolling Mississippi River provides recreation and transportation for communities south of the Twin Cities. On Min-

The Mall of America is located in Bloomington.

Winona is home to the Julius C. Wilkie Steamboat Center.

nesota's eastern border, the scenic Great River Road links Red Wing, the former home of a giant pottery works, with Winona. The highway passes villages, apple orchards, wildlife preserves, fruit stands, craft shops, and bait stores.

Winona stands on a sandbar built up by the Mississippi thousands of years ago. It was founded in 1851 as a steamboat stop and river port. By the 1860s, the city was shipping thousands of tons of wheat and millions of board feet of lumber each year. The Julius C. Wilkie Steamboat Center near the river brings that era back to life. Winona's geography has inspired several legendary tales. Local lore says that an American Indian girl named We-No-Nah leaped from the 500-foot (153-m) bluffs above the river to her death after she was forbidden to marry her sweetheart. Overlooking Winona is Sugar Loaf Mountain, said to be the cap of the legendary Chief Wa-pa-sha, who according to legend turned to stone after he died. Over the years, much of the rocky hill has been quarried.

Rochester is the largest city in southern Minnesota. In the 1850s, pioneers from Rochester, New York, settled here and named it for their hometown. The city is known for its hospitals and clinics. In 1863, during the Civil War, Dr. William Mayo arrived in Rochester to care for Union soldiers. His two sons, William and Charles, followed in their father's footsteps, and in 1889, the three doctors started the Mayo Clinic. Today, patients from around the world visit the internationally famous medical center.

Patients from all over the world come to Rochester's Mayo Clinic.

To the south, on the state's border with Iowa, are the major farming-industrial communities of Austin and Albert Lea. On the Cedar River, Austin was incorporated in 1876 as county seat of Mower County. Albert Lea, at the junction of Interstates 90 and 35, was incorporated in 1878 as county seat of adjacent Freeborn County. Both cities have an interesting mix of grain elevators and modern offices.

CHAPTER SEVEN

A Progressive Government

The state capitol in
St. Paul

Minnesota has always been known for its progressive
government. The state's 1858 constitution has been regularly amended to keep up with the times. The task is not easy,
however.

To amend the constitution, a majority of both houses of the
state legislature must endorse the proposal. Then a majority of voters in a general election must support it. The constitution can also
be amended by a constitutional convention. Two-thirds of the legislature and a majority of the voters in an election can call for such
a convention. Proposals made during a convention become law if
three-fifths of the participating voters approve. This constitution is
Minnesota's basic law, outlining the rights and responsibilities of
its citizens and elected officers.

On the federal level, Minnesota has eight members in the
U.S. House of Representatives, two U.S. senators, and ten elec-

The state capitol in
St. Paul

Opposite: Inside the
state capitol

Former pro wrestler Jesse Ventura was elected governor in 1998.

toral votes in presidential elections. Like the federal government, Minnesota has three separate and independent branches of state government: executive, legislative, and judicial.

The Executive Branch

The state governor, assisted by the lieutenant governor, heads the executive branch. They are elected together on a single-party ticket for four-year terms. A governor can be reelected unlimited times. Minnesota has never elected a female governor.

The governor appoints department directors and members of administrative boards and commissions who usually serve from two to six years. These agencies handle the day-to-day operations of government, ranging from overseeing transportation to protecting natural resources. The governor can also veto legislation and cut appropriation bills. Other elected officials in the executive branch are the secretary of state, auditor, treasurer, and attorney general.

The Legislators

The legislative branch is composed of a state senate and a state house of representatives. Minnesota has 67 state senators who are elected for four-year terms and 134 state representatives who are elected for two-year terms. For many years, state legislators were

Minnesota's Governors

Name	Party	Term	Name	Party	Term
Henry H. Sibley	Dem.	1858–1860	Jacob A. O. Preus	Rep.	1921–1925
Alexander Ramsey	Rep.	1860–1863	Theodore Christianson	Rep.	1925–1931
Henry A. Swift	Rep.	1863–1864	Floyd B. Olson	Farm.-Lab.	1931–1936
Stephen Miller	Rep.	1864–1866	Hjalmar Petersen	Farm.-Lab.	1936–1937
William R. Marshall	Rep.	1866–1870	Elmer A. Benson	Farm.-Lab.	1937–1939
Horace Austin	Rep.	1870–1874	Harold E. Stassen	Rep.	1939–1943
Cushman K. Davis	Rep.	1874–1876	Edward J. Thye	Rep.	1943–1947
John S. Pillsbury	Rep.	1876–1882	Luther W. Youngdahl	Rep.	1947–1951
Lucius F. Hubbard	Rep.	1882–1887	C. Elmer Anderson	Rep.	1951–1955
Andrew R. McGill	Rep.	1887–1889	Orville L. Freeman	DFL*	1955–1961
William R. Merriam	Rep.	1889–1893	Elmer L. Andersen	Rep.	1961–1963
Knute Nelson	Rep.	1893–1895	Karl F. Rolvaag	DFL*	1963–1967
David M. Clough	Rep.	1895–1899	Harold E. LeVander	Rep.	1967–1971
John Lind	Dem.	1899–1901	Wendell R. Anderson	DFL*	1971–1976
Samuel R. Van Sant	Rep.	1901–1905	Rudy Perpich	DFL*	1976–1979
John A. Johnson	Dem.	1905–1909	Albert H. Quie	Ind. Rep.	1979–1983
Adolph O. Eberhart	Rep.	1909–1915	Rudy Perpich	DFL*	1983–1991
Winfield S. Hammond	Dem.	1915	Arne H. Carlson	Ind. Rep.	1991–1999
Joseph A. A. Burnquist	Rep.	1915–1921	Jesse Ventura	Reform	1999–

*Democratic-Farmer-Labor

not allowed to represent a political party, although they didn't hide their liberal or conservative leanings. As of 1974, legislators could declare a party affiliation.

The legislators develop the laws that govern Minnesota. To override the governor's veto requires the support of two-thirds of the members of each house. The Minnesota legislature begins meeting on the Tuesday after the first Monday in January in odd-

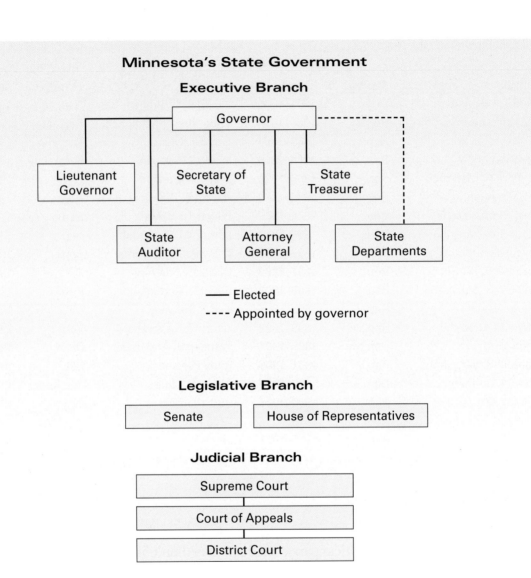

Minnesota's State Government

Executive Branch

Governor

Lieutenant Governor

Secretary of State

State Treasurer

State Auditor

Attorney General

State Departments

—— Elected

---- Appointed by governor

Legislative Branch

Senate | House of Representatives

Judicial Branch

Supreme Court

Court of Appeals

District Court

numbered years. The state's constitution says that regular legislative sessions are not to exceed 120 days over a two-year period. However, the governor can call a special session if in his or her opinion there is a pressing need.

The Humphreys—A Political Family

Hubert H. Humphrey (1911–1978) was one of Minnesota's most famous political leaders. After serving in several federal posts, he was elected mayor of Minneapolis in 1945. Under his administration, the city adopted the nation's first fair employment act, opening the door for women and minorities to get better jobs and higher pay.

Humphrey, a Democratic liberal who advocated civil rights, was elected to the U.S. Senate in 1948. In 1964, he ran for vice president on the Democratic ticket with Lyndon B. Johnson. After President Johnson decided not to run again because of opposition to his Vietnam War policies, Humphrey won the Democratic presidential nomination in 1968. He narrowly lost the race to Republican Richard M. Nixon.

Humphrey's son, Hubert H. Humphrey III (above), has continued the family tradition of government service. In 1982, he was elected attorney general. Since 1994, Humphrey has sought damages from U.S. tobacco companies to reimburse the state for the treatment of patients with smoking-related problems. In 1998, he won a multimillion-dollar settlement that will be used to provide medical care for smokers.

In 1998, Humphrey and Republican candidate Norm Coleman ran for governor. They lost to former professional wrestler and talk-show host Jesse Ventura, a Reform candidate. ▧

A Conservationist Legislator

Hannah Kempfer, born in 1907, came to Minnesota from Norway when she was six years old. As a child in northwestern Otter Tail County, she trapped and hunted to earn money for school. After becoming a teacher, she decided to run for political office. Kempfer was one of four women elected to the 1944 state legislature.

A conservationist, Kempfer represented the rural interests. During her eighteen years as a state legislator, she supported hunting and fishing regulations to preserve Minnesota's wilderness.

Hannah Kempfer was finally defeated after sponsoring a law that required state residents to buy fishing licenses. The measure eventually passed and now the license fees support natural-resource programs in the state. She died in 1966. ■

The State Courts

The state judiciary is headed by the supreme court, with one chief justice and six associate justices who hear appeals from the lower courts. Civil and criminal cases in Minnesota are handled by 254 judges in ten judicial districts. Judges are elected for six-year terms and do not belong to any political party.

In 1982, Minnesota adopted a constitutional amendment that set up a court of appeals. This court consists of sixteen judges elected for six-year terms and helps relieve the supreme court's heavy caseload.

Local Governments

Minnesota has eighty-seven counties. A five-person board of commissioners manages most counties, although some heavily populated counties have added members. Board members are elected to

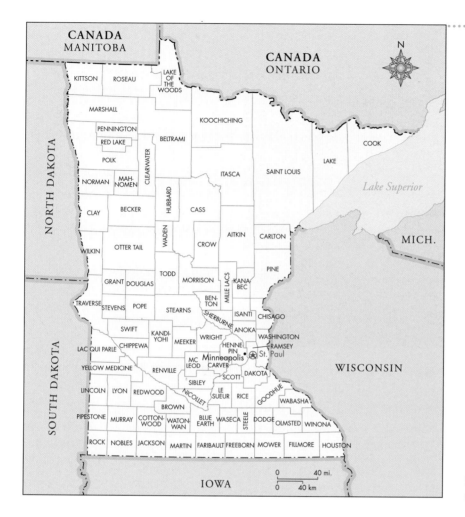

Map of Minnesota's counties

four-year terms. The boards collect taxes and borrow money to pay for projects that improve the quality of life.

The state has more than 850 cities today. According to the state constitution, each city chooses its type of local government. Most cities have mayors and city councils, but some have commissions or council-manager systems. The state also has about 1,800 townships. Each township is governed by a board of supervisors elected to three-year terms at annual meetings.

Minnesota's State Symbols

State bird: Loon This diving waterbird (above), adopted in 1961, gets its name from a Norwegian word meaning "wild, sad cry." The loon is commonly found in Minnesota's lakes.

State fish: Walleye This popular catch was adopted as the state fish in 1965. It is found in lakes all over the state, but most often in northern Minnesota.

State flower: Pink and white lady's slipper Adopted in 1893, this rare flower can be found in wetlands. It is illegal to pick a pink and white lady's slipper, which can grow to be 4 feet (122 cm) tall and live for fifty years.

State gemstone: Lake Superior agate This red-and-orange-banded stone is formed from iron ore found in northern Minnesota. It was adopted in 1969.

State grain: Wild rice This grain is a major industry in Minnesota, which once produced the world's supply of wild rice. Adopted in 1977, it is harvested from lakes where it grows naturally, but farmers sometimes plant it.

State mushroom: Morel Adopted in 1984, this springtime mushroom is found in many parts of the state.

State tree: Norway (or red) pine This stately tree stands in many of the state's forests, including Itasca State Forest, home to a 300-year-old Norway pine. Adopted in 1945, this tree can grow up to 60 to 100 feet (18 to 30 m) tall.

State drink: Milk This beverage was adopted in 1984 as a reminder of its importance to Minnesota's economy.

State muffin: Blueberry Minnesota's rich supply of wild blueberries inspired the adoption of an official state muffin in 1988. ■

Minnesota's State Flag and Seal

The Minnesota state flag, with a version of the state seal in the center, was adopted in 1957. The three dates on the flag represent the year of Minnesota's first permanent settlement (1819), the year of statehood (1858), and the year the original flag was adopted (1893).

The first state seal of Minnesota, based on the seal used during territorial days, was adopted in 1858. It has been revised three times. The state seal combines symbols of Minnesota's agriculture (a man plows a field in the foreground), lumber industry (a tree stump), and Indian heritage (an American Indian on horseback in the background). The state motto, *L'Etoile du Nord* (The Star of the North), runs across the top of the seal. ■

Minnesota's State Song
"Hail! Minnesota"

Words by Truman E. Rickard and Arthur E. Upson (1904)
Music by Truman E. Rickard

The song was originally the University of Minnesota's official hymn. The state legislature made it the official state song in 1945. The only modification is in the second line where "college dear" was changed to "Hail to thee, our State so dear!"

Hail! Minnesota
Minnesota, hail to thee,
Hail to thee, our State so dear.
Thy light shall ever be
A beacon bright and clear.
Thy sons and daughters true
Will proclaim thee near and far.
They will guard thy fame

And adore thy name,
Thou shalt be their Northern Star.
Like the stream that bends to sea,
Like the pine that seeks the blue,
Minnesota, still for thee

Thy sons are strong and true!
From their woods and waters fair,
From their prairies waving far.
At thy call they throng
With their shout and song
Hailing thee, their Northern Star!

Minnesota voters have a Democratic tradition but often back Republican candidates.

Raising Revenue

The state of Minnesota raises about 60 percent of its income through taxes. Federal programs supply the rest. A tax on personal income is deducted from workers' paychecks. Minnesota also has fuel, sales, and corporate income taxes and charges for motor-vehicle licenses. The state brings in about $10.5 billion and spends around $10 billion annually. The government is responsible for police and fire protection, public education, welfare, and the state's highways, bridges, and hospitals.

Political Tussles

Minnesota citizens have always enjoyed a good political tussle. In fact, although the state has a long Democratic tradition, it often votes Republican. Between 1858 and 1931, Minnesota elected only four Democratic governors. In 1932, Franklin D. Roosevelt became the first Democrat to capture the state's electoral votes in a presidential election.

Minnesotans have often gone against the political mold to form nontraditional political organizations, such as the Nonpartisan League. One of its leaders was a lawyer named Charles A. Lindbergh, the son of Swedish immigrants and father of the famous aviator. The Nonpartisan League supported Lindbergh for governor in 1918.

Opponents branded Lindbergh a traitor for his belief that the banking system had pressured the United States into war with Germany. They shot at the political leader and hanged straw dummies of him around the state. Nineteen counties refused to allow the Nonpartisan League to hold public meetings within their borders. But Lindbergh and his supporters continued their efforts, advocating extensive government ownership of public utilities and transportation.

Elmer A. Benson, one of Minnesota's progressive governors

In 1918, the Farmer-Labor Party, a coalition of grain farmers and trade-union activists, formed as a successor to the Nonpartisan League. Germans and members of other ethnic groups whose loyalty was unfairly questioned during World War I joined the new party.

The Farmer-Labor Party quickly became a powerful vote-getting machine and grew even stronger during the Great Depression of the 1930s when the state economy collapsed. During those hard times, angry and out-of-work voters left the Republican Party in droves. They turned to progressive governors Floyd B. Olson, Hjalmar Petersen, and Elmer A. Benson.

The traditional Democratic Party and the Farmer-Labor Party joined forces in 1944 to form the Democratic-Farmer-Labor Party (DFL). In 1975, the Republican Party of Minnesota changed its name to the Independent Republicans of Minnesota. Regardless of affiliation, most Minnesotans take their responsibilities as citizens seriously and turn out for even minor elections.

CHAPTER EIGHT

Timber, Wheat, and Tourism

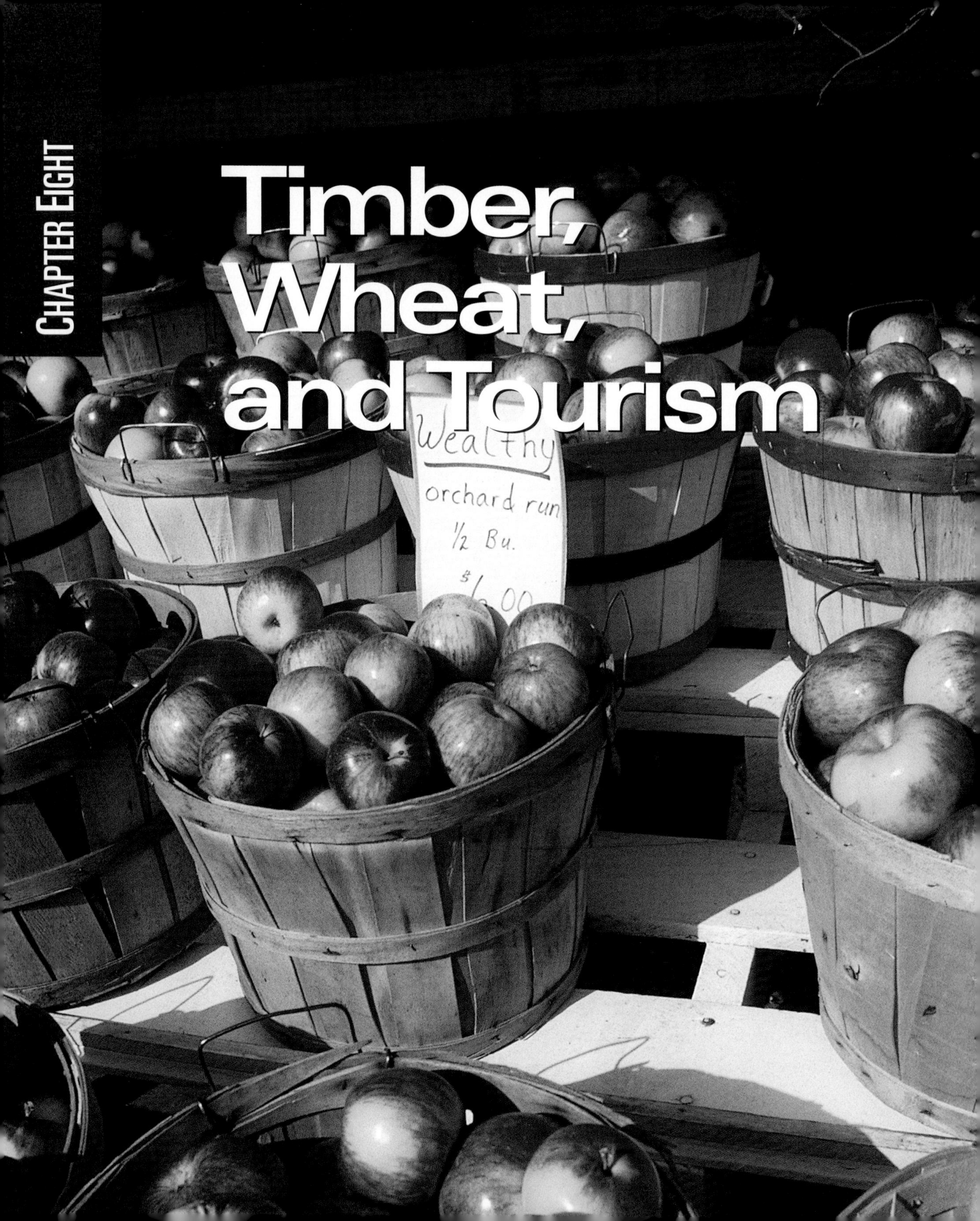

Wealthy

orchard run

½ Bu.

$6.00

3M headquarters

A great variety of goods and services sustains Minnesota's economy. The state has a strong wholesale and retail trade sector and vigorous financial, insurance, and real estate businesses. Two of the largest U.S. retail stores, Dayton Hudson and Super Valu, have their headquarters in the Twin Cities. Also headquartered in the Twin Cities is the Minnesota Mining and Manufacturing Company (3M), which began producing cellophane tape in 1930. Advertising executives, lawyers, accountants, and other professionals support these industries.

Minnesota's diversified manufacturing generates $25 billion a year. Businesses produce a range of items from medical equipment to computers. The publishing industry produces books, newspapers, and at least 550 periodicals.

Coal-fired power plants provide 65 percent of the energy needed to keep the economy running. The state also has two nuclear power plants and several plants that burn petroleum. Minnesota buys some of its electric power from other U.S. states and Canada.

True to its agricultural heritage, Minnesota is a national leader in canning and freezing fresh vegetables, producing flour and breakfast cereal, and growing rice. While some farmers cultivate wild rice on plantations, some Ojibwa harvest rice in the traditional

Opposite: Apples from Minnesota orchards

manner. Native Americans float their canoes into a rice bed, where they use heavy sticks, or knockers, to knock the rice grains from the stalks into the bottom of the canoe. Then they take the rice grains to a central drier for cleaning and preparation.

Minnesota also has a successful poultry industry, with several large plants in Austin and Albert Lea. Poultry-processing facilities work around the clock in central Minnesota. King Turkey Day festival in Worthington has become so popular that movie stars and politicians have joined the celebration.

From apples to timber, the state's rich renewable natural resources are a valuable asset. Minnesota's farm sales total almost $7 billion a year. Sugar beets, corn, flax, barley, and soybeans are among the principal commodities. About 150 apple orchards are scattered across the state, mostly around the Twin Cities and along the Mississippi River. Apple growers produce more than thirty varieties, including McIntosh, Red Delicious, Prairie Spy, and Keepsake. Researchers at the University of Minnesota developed the Haralson, a tart, crunchy apple, in 1920 and the Honey Crisp in 1960.

Wheat—A Familiar Business

When Minnesotans talk wheat, they know their business. Semitrailer trucks pull up next to the harvesting machinery in the fields and load up to 750 bushels. Drivers transport the cargo directly to farm centers such as Hastings, where a row of storage towers holds 17 million bushels of freshly harvested wheat and rye. The silos, 60 to 80 feet (18 to 24 m) tall, can store from 26,000 to 32,000 bushels apiece. On the tracks, Soo Line Railroad's gray hopper cars carry at least 3,300 bushels each.

Wild Rice Soup

Wild rice is a major product of Minnesota. Wild rice dishes are state specialties.

Ingredients:

- 1/2 cup Minnesota wild rice
- 2½ cups water
- 4 cups chicken stock
- 2 tablespoons butter
- 1/4 cup minced onion
- 1/4 cup flour
- 1/2 teaspoon salt
- 1/4 cup grated carrots
- 1/4 cup diced celery
- 1 pint half-and-half

Directions:

Rinse rice thoroughly. Combine water and rice in a saucepan. Bring to a boil. Reduce heat and simmer for 45–60 minutes. Cover and let stand for 5 minutes. Drain any excess water.

Heat chicken stock, then set it aside.

Melt the butter in a saucepan and sauté onion until the onion becomes transparent. Slowly stir in the flour. Then slowly stir in the chicken stock. Keep stirring until the mixture starts to thicken. Stir in the cooked rice, and then add the salt, carrots, and celery. Simmer for 5 minutes.

Stir in the half-and-half. Heat the soup until it's hot enough to serve.

Serves 4–6.

Wheat is one of the state's main crops.

Other cities in Minnesota have similar storage and grinding facilities. For instance, Duluth's six oldest grain elevators, more than 100 feet (30.5 m) tall, hold more than 1 million bushels of grain apiece. In Duluth Harbor, Harvest States Cooperatives owns a more modern elevator that can store up to 18 million bushels. Duluth unloads thousands of grain-filled railcars each year. Modern machinery can empty a 3,600-bushel hopper car in ninety seconds. The Seaway Port Authority of Duluth supervises all wheat loading and other port activity.

The Minnesota Department of Agriculture has many programs to help farmers manage their land. There are waste-pesticide collection programs, conservation plans, and chemical cleanup pro-

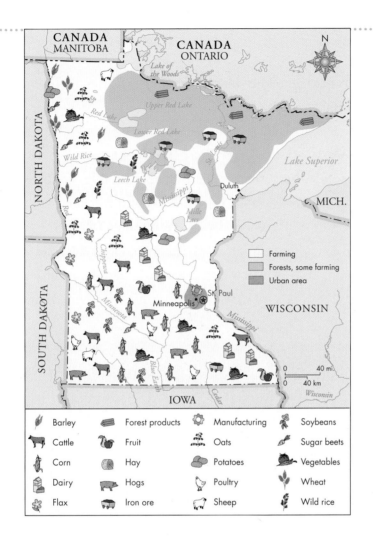

Wheat Milling

The Con Agra complex in Hastings consists of five mills. The two used for hard wheat are able to grind 25 bushels a minute. One mill grinds durham wheat, used for making pasta, at 12 bushels a minute. Another mill grinds whole wheat or rye at 2.5 bushels a minute. The work goes on 24 hours a day, 350 days a year, and produces about 2.5 million pounds (1.1 million kg) of flour a day. ■

Minnesota's natural resources

Map legend:
- Farming
- Forests, some farming
- Urban area

Map symbols:
- Barley
- Cattle
- Corn
- Dairy
- Flax
- Forest products
- Fruit
- Hay
- Hogs
- Iron ore
- Manufacturing
- Oats
- Potatoes
- Poultry
- Sheep
- Soybeans
- Sugar beets
- Vegetables
- Wheat
- Wild rice

What Minnesota Grows, Manufactures, and Mines

Agriculture
Beef cattle
Corn
Hogs
Milk
Soybeans
Wheat
Wild rice

Manufacturing
Electrical equipment
Food products
Forest products
Machinery
Printed materials
Scientific instruments

Mining
Iron ore

jects to ensure that the state's farmlands will remain productive for generations to come.

The Valuable Lumber Industry

Minnesota's thick forests have been valuable since lumbering began in the 1830s. Logs were cut in the forests and floated down the rivers to mills, where they were trimmed into planks. Loggers worked in winter because it was easier to carry the trees out of the woods on sleds over the frozen bogs. When the river ice melted, tens of thousands of logs marked with the owner's brand rushed

Logging has a long history in Minnesota.

The Birth of a Lumber Dynasty

In 1856, when he was seventeen years old, Frederick Weyerhaeuser (right) immigrated to the United States from Germany with his family. He started out working in a small lumber mill in Rock Island, Illinois. Weyerhaeuser saved his money and eventually bought that small mill and then other mills. To supply logs for his lumbering production, he bought timberland in Minnesota and Wisconsin.

In 1891, Frederick Weyerhaeuser moved his home and offices to St. Paul. The company he founded remains one of the largest timber operations in North America. ■

downstream. Today, about 330 million board feet (792,000 cu m) of lumber, along with 5 million Christmas trees, are cut annually.

After the timber companies finished their work, they left a wasteland of brush and stumps—a serious fire hazard. The Hinckley Fire of September 1, 1894, which erupted in the dry woods and swept over the town, was one of the most tragic. It covered 480 square miles (1,243 sq km) and killed more than 400 people before finally dying out.

Such calamities did not deter the lumber companies, which continued to hire hundreds of men to cut timber each season. Lumberjacks earned only $1.50 a day, including meals and a bunk. By the turn of the century, there were at least 350 "jack camps" in the Minnesota woods. Each had a bunkhouse, a cookhouse, a store, a blacksmith shop, and storage buildings. A typical lumber camp is on display at the Forest History Center in Grand Rapids.

Today, the Forestry Department of the Minnesota Department of Natural Resources helps manage the state's timber resources. Timber companies have been replanting trees to ensure future crops. The state now has more trees than it did in 1900.

Lumbering and the manufacture of wood products is the state's second-largest industry and employs 59,000 people. Products made from Minnesota's trees include plywood, baseball bats, toothpicks, nutcrackers, hockey sticks, chopsticks, fishing poles, chessboards, baskets, bird feeders, and windmill blades.

Minnesota Mining

Minnesota remains the nation's top producer of iron ore. In the mid-1990s, the state mined, processed, and shipped almost 47.4 million tons of ore each year.

In 1890, a teamster who worked for a local lumberman named Leonidas Merritt got stuck in some heavy red earth near the village of Tower on the Vermilion Range northeast of the Mesabi Range.

Leave the Driving to Greyhound

Intercity bus service got its start in Minnesota in 1914 when a shrewd young man named Carl Wickman bought a large touring car and began ferrying people between the town of Hibbing and the nearby mines in northern Minnesota. Wickman and partner Andrew Anderson charged fifteen cents for a ride on "Bus Andy." Business was so profitable they had a real bus built and expanded their transportation service to other towns in Minnesota's Iron Range. Later, the company moved to Duluth and started statewide routes under the name of Greyhound Lines. Today, Greyhound is the largest U.S. interstate passenger carrier. ■

The workman, who knew about minerals, had the dirt tested. He and his boss discovered the sample was full of iron. Merritt and his brothers soon opened up their own mining business.

Mining required a large investment. Big businessmen from the East Coast, including John D. Rockefeller, J. P. Morgan, and Andrew Carnegie, were among the first to invest heavily in Minnesota's lucrative mining operations. They supplied the money to lay the railroad tracks that transport Minnesota's ore and to build the piers for the ships that carry the ore. They also owned the trains, ships, and iron smelters. Duluth profited from the resulting mining boom, and as long as the money flowed, nobody cared who was underwriting the operations.

A taconite mine in Fairchild

The port of Duluth is busy throughout the year.

Today, the port of Duluth serves more than 1,200 vessels a year, 200 of which are foreign. The "salties," or oceangoing ships, are more than 1,000 feet (305 m) long and carry up to 68,000 tons of cargo.

The port's Dock Number Six can stockpile up to 3 million tons of taconite iron ore, which is enough to fill fifty freighters

1,000 feet (305 m) long. Owned by the Duluth, Missabe, and Iron Range Railway, the dock is 2,304 feet (703 m) long and 85 feet (26 m) tall and one of the largest ore-loading facilities on the Great Lakes. The dock can unload four trains every eight hours on its three tracks. The cars dump the ore through holes into the dock's storage bins. Each of the dock pockets holds about 280 tons. To fill a 1,000-foot (305-m) freighter, 875 trainloads are required. The job takes about seven hours. Thanks to computer technology, managing the maze of conveyer belts that load the taconite requires only seventy employees.

Commerce-Friendly Associations

Numerous state agencies and private organizations help Minnesota's large corporations and small businesses. The Red River Trade Corridor in Minnesota's upper northwest, for example, economically links the state with the Dakotas and the Canadian province of Manitoba. Since its formation in 1989, the group has developed new industry, pushed for better transportation connections, and promoted high-tech telecommunications.

Eighteen employer associations and chambers of commerce work together through the Coalition of Minnesota Businesses to educate the broader community about the importance of manufacturing and trade. Minnesota Technology, Inc., links companies with educators and researchers to help the state's businesses stay up-to-date and competitive.

Minnesota businesses are eager to expand their opportunities internationally. The state already ships many products to Latin America, Europe, Asia, and Australia. The state's leading trade partners outside the United States are Canada, Japan, Great Britain, Germany, the Netherlands, and Thailand. Minnesota ranks among the top five states in the export of agricultural products such as soybeans, dairy items, wheat, and vegetables. Trade delegations from other countries often visit Minnesota to see the latest in farming and manufacturing. Minnesota businesspeople also travel overseas regularly to market their wares.

The Thriving Industry of Tourism

Minnesota welcomes more than 20 million visitors a year. Tourists flock to the Museum of Questionable Medical Devices in Minneapolis, Artfest in Albert Lea, the Fishermen's Picnic in Grand Marais, the Minnesota Finlandia Ski Marathon in Bemidji, and performances of the St. Paul Chamber Orchestra. Visitors pump $9.1 billion into Minnesota's economy every year. The tourism industry employs about 170,300 Minnesotans in positions that range from hotel desk clerk to motor-coach-company president.

Opposite: A crowd enjoying the Minnesota Renaissance Festival in Shakopee

CHAPTER NINE

A Diverse Group

Minnesotans live in cities and small towns, in suburbs, and on farms. They may be named Svenborg, Shaskey, Wronka, Schmidt, Russell, Conley, Shariff, Vang, Little Thunder, Smyth, or Gunderson. They may be Lutheran, Roman Catholic, Greek Orthodox, Muslim, Jewish, Hindu, or Baptist or they may have no religious affiliation at all. They or their ancestors may have emigrated from England, Scotland, Germany, Denmark, Norway, Canada, Poland, Iceland, Ireland, Wales, France, Italy, Sweden, Russia, Cuba, Ethiopia, Finland, Thailand, Vietnam, Lebanon, Mexico, Guatemala, Korea, or Ecuador. Minnesota's national heritage reads like a United Nations roster.

The Scottish Country Fair is just one of Minnesota's ethnic festivals.

All Minnesotans have ancestors who were immigrants. Even the first American Indians originated outside the region and came to the area to hunt wild game or in search of uninhabited land.

The largest number of immigrants came to Minnesota beginning in the 1830s. By the turn of the century, the Norwegians, Swedes, Danes, and Finns who lived in Minnesota outnumbered those from any other part of Europe. The state's forests, lakes, hills,

Opposite: Cross-country skiing on Gunflint Trail

People from all over the world have come to live in Minnesota.

and valleys reminded Scandinavians of their homeland. The largest single group of newcomers came from Germany.

African-Americans were in the first group of traders and trappers. More moved to the state during the Civil War, with another influx in the 1930s. The 1990 census counted 94,944 African-American residents in the state.

Mexican families settled in Minnesota during the 1920s. At first, most were migrant workers who followed the seasons to pick and harvest crops. Eventually, they settled into permanent homes, established churches, and opened businesses. Their success led to the emigration of other Spanish speakers from Central and South America and the Caribbean. In the 1990 census, 53,884 Minnesotans were of Spanish-speaking heritage, an increase of 70 percent since 1980.

In the mid-1980s, numerous refugees came to Minnesota from Vietnam, Cambodia, and Laos. The 1990 census recorded 77,886 residents from Asia and the Pacific Islands, an increase of 193 percent since 1980.

Helping the Newcomers

Immigrants have had to adjust to living in unfamiliar surroundings. Some have changed their language, food, customs, and clothing easily, and others have benefited from assistance. Some immigrants didn't take long to make their mark. For example, Rudolph

The State's First Church

Minnesota's first church was a 25-foot (7.6-m)-long log cabin constructed in 1841 by five Catholic French-Canadians named Le Bissoniere, Gervais, Bottineau, Morin, and Geurin. ■

(Rudy) Perpich, the son of an immigrant miner from Hibbing, became Minnesota's governor in 1976.

Associations such as Duluth's International Institute and the statewide Catholic Social Services help people make the cultural transition. Fraternal groups meet in halls and churches, hold picnics and dances, and share their memories. Slovenes, Irish, Ukrainians, and other nationalities have social clubs. The Norwegian-American Historical Association and the American Swedish Institute keep a record of the past in publications and exhibits.

Minnesotans have always been ready and eager to help the newest arrivals. In 1892, when a trainload of Russian Jews fleeing persecution in their homeland arrived in St. Paul, many local residents helped them find homes and jobs.

Another example is Constance Currie, who came to St. Paul's close-knit west-side neighborhood in 1918 and ran Neighborhood House, a local service agency, for the next thirty-nine years. Currie was the U.S. delegate to a world conference on settlement work in 1931 and received an honor from the Mexican government for helping the city's Mexican Americans.

Latest Surge of Immigrants

About 18,000 Hmong people from Laos, in Southeast Asia, make up the latest surge of arrivals. More than 50,000 of these hill people settled in Minnesota, fleeing their homes after helping the United States fight the Vietnam War. They used their farming expertise to provide produce for farmers' markets. Their weaving and hand stitching are often considered works of art. In 1992,

Population of Minnesota's Major Cities (1990)

Minneapolis	368,383
St. Paul	272,235
Bloomington	86,335
Duluth	85,493
Rochester	70,745
Brooklyn Park	56,381

How Many Minnesotans?

The 1990 U.S. census counted 4,387,029 Minnesota residents, rising to an estimated 4,682,748 in 1996. Most of the Minnesota population is between twenty-two and sixty-two years old. More than 16,000 families consist of seven or more people. ■

Many Hmong people
came to Minnesota
after the Vietnam War.

Choua Lee became the first Hmong American elected to U.S. public office as a member of the St. Paul school board.

The Wilder Foundation's Social Adjustment Project for Southeast Asians and the Center for Hmong Adolescent Development in St. Paul are organizations that help Asian youngsters adjust to their surroundings. Such agencies encourage young people not to use drugs or join gangs. The groups also work with parents. Because each generation looks at the world differently, opposing viewpoints can cause conflict at home.

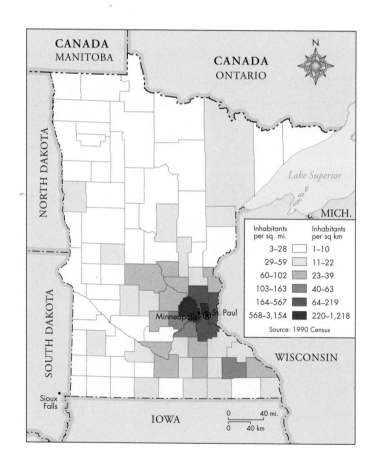

Minnesota's
population density

Clashes of Cultures

Historically, newcomers have brought their beliefs and ethics with them to Minnesota. Among the many Scandinavian émigrés were Finnish socialists who believed in community ownership of utilities and transportation. They demanded better working conditions in the Iron Range mines and helped organize a dockworkers' strike in Duluth in 1913. Their hard-fought efforts forced shipping management to improve safety in the port.

The Ojibwa tribe is one of the Native American groups living in Minnesota.

Even today, however, traditions sometimes clash. Under the terms of a now-controversial 1837 treaty, several Ojibwa groups in northern Minnesota wanted to spear and net for walleyes in lakes near their homes as their ancestors had done for hundreds of years. Because many people outside the Indian community did not understand their traditional ways, the Ojibwa requests sparked lawsuits and demonstrations over the fear that too many fish would be caught in a single season. To ensure that overfishing did not occur in 1998, the Ojibwas' own natural resource experts worked with the state to set bag limits and track the catches. Governor Arne Carlson and other state leaders appealed for calm and, for the most part, the problem was resolved peacefully.

Lawrence Taliaferro— Promoter of Peace

In the past, during conflicts between the U.S. government and Native American tribes, Indian agents worked for the United States as negotiators. While some agents cheated the Indians under their supervision, most were hardworking and honest. One of the best was Lawrence Taliaferro (1794–1871). Taliaferro came to Minnesota from Virginia in 1819 and was known for getting along with both the Dakota and Ojibwa and encouraging them to keep peace between the groups. ■

Living a Traditional Life in Minnesota

Amish families live throughout southeastern Minnesota and farm with horse and plow just as their ancestors did in the 1700s. Preferring more traditional ways of living, they don't use electricity or drive cars. Dressed in their basic black clothing, youngsters often sell homemade bread, jams, and cookies along the roadside. Akin to the Pennsylvania Dutch, the Amish are a religious sect that originated in Germany. ■

A High Value on Education

Whatever their background, Minnesotans value education. They know it helps them get jobs and move ahead in their lives. Children between the ages of seven and sixteen are required to attend school. Some schools allow pupils to work as apprentices to learn firsthand about various professions.

The Minnesota Department of Children, Families, and Learning supervises the state's school districts. The governor, with approval from the state senate, appoints a commissioner to a four-

Education is important to the Minnesotan way of life.

year term. A state board of education, consisting of nine members, sets education goals. The governor, again with approval of the senate, also appoints these officials for four-year terms. Each local school board is managed by an elected school board.

During the 1998–1999 school year, there were 382,659 elementary school pupils and 399,625 high school children in Minnesota at 975 elementary, 154 middle, and 462 high schools. Minnesota also has 537 private elementary and high schools, usually affiliated with a religious denomination. There were 47,586 elementary and 28,619 high school pupils attending these schools in 1997–1998.

Institutions of Higher Learning

Minnesota has sixty-two public and forty-four private institutions of higher learning. The state-run University of Minnesota, established in 1851, has colleges of liberal arts, technology, natural resources, education, pharmacy, law, dentistry, and biological sci-

The University of Minnesota in winter

Minnesota's First Schools

In the early 1820s, the first school for white children opened for the families of officers and soldiers at Fort St. Anthony (later renamed Fort Snelling). In the 1830s, missionary priests established schools for American Indian children. In 1849, the territorial legislature passed a law to establish public schools. In 1851, the job of a territorial superintendent of schools was established.

ences as well as schools of medicine, management, nursing, and dentistry. Its main campus is located in the Twin Cities, with branches in Duluth, Morris, and Crookston.

The state also has many excellent private colleges and universities, including the Minneapolis College of Art and Design, Carleton, St. Catherine's, Macalester, Hamline, St. Mary's, St. Benedict's, St. John's, St. Thomas, St. Olaf, and Gustavus Adolphus. Many are rooted in the Catholic or Lutheran traditions. Some of these institutions offer programs for younger people. For instance, Concordia College in Moorhead has a "Dr. Physics" program on the Internet designed to teach kids from kindergarten through high school about the physical world.

The University of St. Thomas is located in St. Paul.

Libraries—Public and Private

Minnesota's 330 public libraries, with outreach programs for young readers, are important resources. The Hennepin County system, one of the largest in the United States, circulates more than 10 million items annually. There are also many specialty libraries. The Minnesota Historical Society's Library in St. Paul, Rochester's Mayo Medical Library, and the State Law Library are first-rate sources of historical and up-to-date information.

A Minnesotan Educator

William Watts Folwell (1833–1929) was the first president of the University of Minnesota. Born in New York, he moved to Minnesota in 1869. He was a leader in developing innovative programs for high schools and set up a unified system of public education. Folwell also wrote a comprehensive history of early Minnesota. ■

CHAPTER TEN

"Where All the Women Are Strong . . ."

M innesota is home to dozens of remarkable writers, and many have written about their childhood in the Gopher State. They include journalist and author Harrison Salisbury, actress and short-story writer Meridel Le Sueur, novelists Jon Hassler and Patricia Hampl, poets Robert Bly, Shirley Schoonover, and Keith Gunderson, and African-American essayist Toyse Kysle. Minnesotan writers for young readers include Carol Ryrie Brink, author of the award-winning *Caddie Woodlawn*, and writers and illustrators Wanda Gag (*Millions of Cats*) and Nancy Carlson.

Robert Bly, one of Minnesota's many writers

One of the most important authors from Minnesota was Sinclair Lewis (1885–1951). His award-winning novel *Main Street* was published in 1920. Folks from his hometown, Sauk Centre, thought he was writing about them when he attacked the snobbishness and prejudice of the era, and many years passed before they accepted him again. Today, the town is proud to be called the "Original Main Street." Lewis was not the first Minnesotan author to write about small-town life. In the 1850s, minister Edward Eggleston wrote a popular novel about a fictional town he called Metropolisville.

Author F. Scott Fitzgerald (1896–1940) was also born in Minnesota. *This Side of Paradise* (1920), his first novel, earned immediate popularity for its depiction of the "Roaring Twenties." Young

Opposite: Minnesota Children's Museum

F. Scott Fitzgerald was born in St. Paul.

people of Fitzgerald's time identified with his characters and sense of style. The novelist's third work, *The Great Gatsby* (1925), which focuses on the excesses of the fast-paced Jazz Age, was a major contribution to American literature. F. Scott Fitzgerald died in Hollywood, California, where he lived while writing film scripts.

Some Minnesotans use their ethnic heritage in their writing. Edna and Howard Hong have published translations of Scandinavian writers and have written about their reflections on growing up in Minnesota. Norwegian-born Ole E. Rolvaag wrote *Giants in the Earth: A Saga of the Prairie* about Norwegian settlers' stark pioneer life in the 1870s; the novel was published in Norwegian in 1925 and in English in 1927. After attending St. Olaf College in Northfield, Rolvaag eventually became head of the college's Norwegian languages and literature department. Ojibwa-French educator-writer Gerald Vizenor, who teaches at the University of California at Berkeley, relates the traditional tales and songs of his people.

Other authors take different creative approaches. Emma Bull, born in California in 1954, came to Minnesota as a freelance journalist in 1976. She and her husband, Will Shetterly, edit fantasy anthologies and are active in a local fiction writers' group called the Scribblies.

Garrison Keillor—A National Personality

Garrison Keillor is a contemporary social commentator and humorist with a familiar and distinctive voice. His radio show, *A Prairie Home Companion*, is a regular feature distributed by Public Radio International and attracts millions of listeners each week.

Keillor says he talks for a hobby. On the show, which started in 1974, Keillor tells stories about the fictional Minnesota town of Lake Wobegon, where "all the women are strong, the men good looking and all the children are above average." *A Prairie Home Companion* is recorded live from the Fitzgerald Theater in St. Paul, but Keillor often takes to the road to broadcast from other cities.

Storyteller, author, poet, and musician, Keillor was born in Anoka, Minnesota, in 1942. He received a bachelor's degree in English from the University of Minnesota in 1966. His first job was working as a classical music broadcaster at Collegeville's KSJN radio—the original station in the state's now multicity public radio network.

A Center for Book Lovers

Bookstores have a special place in Minnesota's literary and cultural scene. The Center for the Book, the Hungry Mind, and the Red Balloon are popular stops for eager readers. The Loft, a writers' center in Minneapolis, offers grants, classes, and public workshops featuring local and international writers. Arise!, another bookstore in Minneapolis, features major political thinkers and writers from the developing world. For kids, the Comic College in Minneapolis offers a large collection of comic books and cartoons. Minnesota is also the home of several publishers of children's books.

A Sound for Everyone

Minnesota also has a vibrant music scene ranging from world-famous symphonies to chamber orchestras and barbershop quartets. There is a sound for everyone. Boiled in Lead sings Irish tunes. Calvin Krime records on the Amphetamine Reptile Records label. Lutheran songwriter Jay Beech performs for youth groups. The Greater Twin Cities Youth Symphony, established in 1972, gives regular concerts.

Famous singers born in Minnesota include folk star Bob Dylan and the musician referred to as the "Artist formerly known as Prince." Dylan, whose real name is Robert Allan Zimmerman, was born on May 24, 1941, and grew up in Hibbing. He attended the University of Minnesota for a time and then left school for New York City's hip Greenwich Village. Dylan's songs spoke to the social and emotional turmoil that his generation experienced. Among them were "The Times They Are A-Changin'," "A Hard Rain's A-Gonna Fall," "Slow Train Comin'," and "Blowin' in the Wind."

The Artist formerly known as Prince was born in Minneapolis as Prince Rogers Nelson on June 7, 1958. At thirteen, he was a guitarist in his first band, Grand Central, started by his cousin, drummer Charles Smith. He went on to write more than 300 songs for himself and about 200 tunes for other artists. He is said to have about 1,000 unreleased compositions. In 1985, the Artist formerly known as Prince started his Paisley Park record label in the Twin Cities and remains a fixture in the community, actively advising and promoting younger musicians.

From *Fargo* to *Fences*

Filmmakers are drawn to Minnesota's lakes, woods, cities, small towns, and interesting people. Several feature films have been made in the state, including the dark, award-winning *Fargo*, the comic *Grumpy Old Men*, and Walt Disney's *Mighty Ducks* series about a scrappy hockey club.

On-location filming takes a lot of planning. Production com-

Musician Bob Dylan grew up in Hibbing.

Emilio Estevez (right) in The Mighty Ducks

panies must obtain licenses, block off streets for outdoor scenes, have police on hand, store equipment, and hire extras. The state-funded Minnesota Film Board works with site locators to find the best places for a film's scenes. It also serves as the liaison between local communities and production companies in handling the million behind-the-scenes details of making a movie.

Everyone loves watching films. The University Film Society at the University of Minnesota was one of the first U.S. nonprofit organizations to show movies from around the world on a regular basis.

Playwright August
Wilson

The state's theaters are also plentiful. The Minneapolis Children's Theatre Company, Tyrone Guthrie Theater, and Dudley Riggs' Brave New Workshop are among the best known. African-American playwright August Wilson moved to Minnesota in the 1970s. In 1987, his play *Fences* became a Broadway hit. His works regularly appear at the Penumbra Theater in St. Paul, one of the world's foremost African-American theaters.

Artists and Artisans

Artists have always been attracted to Minnesota's endlessly fascinating landscapes. Artist Charles Beck painted scenes of Fergus Falls and its surrounding fields generations ago. Another early

Gordon Parks

Born in 1912, Gordon Parks came to Minnesota from Kansas after his mother died when he was sixteen years old. He worked at many odd jobs through the Great Depression to earn money for school. For a time, he was so poor he slept on streetcar benches in the Twin Cities. Gordon Parks finally landed a job with the Civilian Conservation Corps building trails in the woods. He later worked as a waiter on a train that traveled between Minneapolis and Seattle.

On one trip, Parks bought a secondhand camera, and almost immediately knew he had found his calling. In 1948, Gordon Parks became the first African-American photographer at *Life* magazine. He went on to write several books about his life, including *A Choice of Weapons*, and also worked as one of Hollywood's first African-American filmmakers. ■

landscape painter, Adolf Dehn, captured the state's geology in his watercolors.

Most Minnesota communities have a gallery or hall for local artists. The Southeast Minnesota Visual Art Gallery in Rochester and the Minneapolis Institute of Arts regularly feature the state's modern artists. A major exhibit in 1998 at the art institute featured sculptures by Minnesotans Alan Wadzinski, Jan Elftmann, Bill Klaila, Rollin Marquette, Rick Salafia, and Joy Kops.

Minnesota's craft scene is also rich. Weavers express their ethnic traditions in their weaving styles. Bounxou Chanthraphone uses Laotian patterns while Rosemary Roehl emphasizes Norwegian designs. Fishing lures made by Burt Hyatt and John Jensen are appreciated by anglers and art lovers alike. Ojibwa Benjamin Fairbanks constructs beautiful baskets from birch bark.

The state actively helps its artists. The Minnesota Arts Board offers grants and other aid to artists, organizations, and schools. The agency prints numerous publications to help the arts community, including a folk-art guide and listings of gallery space.

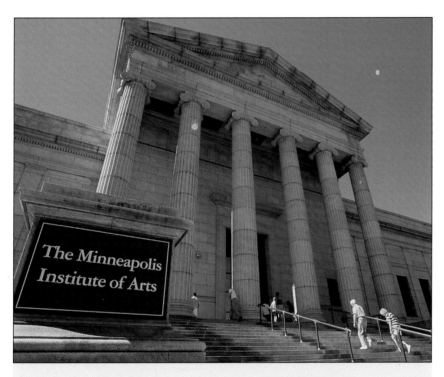

Minnesota's Largest Arts Center

The Minneapolis Institute of Arts hosts 400,000 guests every year. Built in 1915, the arts center recently underwent a massive ten-year expansion and renovation. The structure now covers 8 acres (3.2 ha) and offers thirty-three new gallery spaces, five classrooms, an African Gallery, and an expanded Asian collection. The Institute of Arts' Family Center has computers with art activities at a child's eye level and an activity area with soft sculptures. ■

A Wealth of Museums

Minnesota's youngsters have many museums to explore, from the Minnesota Children's Museum to the Science Museum of Minnesota. Founded in St. Paul in 1907, the Science Museum has a giant-screened Omni theater and special exhibits. There is even the Museum of Questionable Medical Devices in Minneapolis. And then, on the outskirts of the Twin Cities, there's the Minnesota Zoo, where there are few cages, and animals are separated by wide moats.

Sports Stadiums

The Hubert H. Humphrey Metrodome is home to the Minnesota Twins baseball team, which won the World Series championship in 1987 and 1991. The Metrodome also hosts the Minnesota Vikings and the University of Minnesota Golden Gophers football teams. It is the only facility in the United States that has hosted a Super Bowl, a World Series, and an NCAA Final Four Basketball Championship. The National Basketball Association's Timberwolves play at the Target Center. The Minnesota Wild hockey team launched its first season in a new arena in St. Paul in 2000.

Amateur Sports Figures

The state's amateur athletes stay busy. In the early 1990s, Derek Williams set a Big Ten college record for the 100-meter butterfly stroke and was ranked as one of the ten fastest swimmers in the world. Rene Capo is an international judo champion. Dannette Leininger plays team handball. Pete Durben is an Olympic rifleman. And Bob Kempainen is a top-ranked marathon runner.

**Viking quarterback
Randall Cunningham**

Another amateur Minnesota athlete is Kris Kuehl, who threw her first discus when she was in eighth grade—58 feet (18 m). By the time she tried out for the 1996 Olympics, Kuehl was throwing more than 198 feet (60 m). She hopes to break the world record of 216 feet, 10 inches (66 m). The list of Minnesota's amateur sports figures goes on and on.

Winter and Summer Fun

Warm weather brings hikers to Itasca State Park.

Figure skating, hockey, and skiing are the winter sports of choice in Minnesota. In January, the John Beargrease Sled Dog Race

between Duluth and Grand Marais pits men and women and their dogs against the elements. Then comes the annual St. Paul Winter Carnival, which celebrates the season with dances, snow-sculpting competitions, concerts, and a giant parade. Vulcans, dressed like devils to represent the sun's heat, roam the streets in their souped-up vintage fire trucks. At the end of the carnival, the Vulcans win the day in their friendly "battle" with the winter court ruled by Boreas Rex. It is said that a Vulcan victory means the state will enjoy another fun-filled summer.

When the weather warms up in Minnesota, fishing poles come out. Anglers haul in an estimated 35,000 pounds (15,800 kilograms) of game fish each year. Swimming, whitewater rafting, canoeing, hunting, hiking, and off-road biking are other popular summer sports. In June, Grandma's Marathon brings thousands of runners to Duluth. In July and August, Brainerd International Raceway's auto racing attracts visitors from around the world. There is always something to do in the Gopher State.

Timeline

United States History

The first permanent English settlement is established in North America at Jamestown. **1607**

Pilgrims found Plymouth Colony, the second permanent English settlement. **1620**

America declares its independence from Britain. **1776**

The Treaty of Paris officially ends the Revolutionary War in America. **1783**

The U.S. Constitution is written. **1787**

The Louisiana Purchase almost doubles the size of the United States. **1803**

The United States and Britain fight the War of 1812. **1812–15**

Minnesota State History

1654 and 1660 Pierre Radisson and Médard Chouart explore Minnesota.

1679 Daniel Greysolon explores northeastern Minnesota and convinces the Dakota and Ojibwa tribes to recognize King Louis XIV of France as their authority.

1680 Father Louis Hennepin canoes up the Mississippi River and is captured by the Dakota.

1783 Eastern Minnesota is given to the new United States.

1803 Western Minnesota is granted to the United States after the Louisiana Purchase.

1819 Zebulon Pike takes control of the junction of the Minnesota and Mississippi Rivers, where Fort Snelling is eventually established.

1836 Eastern Minnesota becomes part of Wisconsin Territory.

1849 Minnesota Territory is established.

1851 Land west of the Mississippi River is given up by the Sioux.

United States History

The North and South fight **1861–65** each other in the American Civil War.

The United States is **1917–18** involved in World War I.

The stock market crashes, **1929** plunging the United States into the Great Depression.

The United States **1941–45** fights in World War II.

The United States becomes a **1945** charter member of the U.N.

The United States **1951–53** fights in the Korean War.

The U.S. Congress enacts a series of **1964** groundbreaking civil rights laws.

The United States **1964–73** engages in the Vietnam War.

The United States and other **1991** nations fight the brief Persian Gulf War against Iraq.

Minnesota State History

1858 Minnesota becomes a state.

1862 Fighting breaks out in western Minnesota between settlers and the Dakota. Construction begins on the Minnesota & Pacific Railroad.

1884 Iron ore is first shipped from the Vermilion Range in northern Minnesota.

1889 The Mayo Clinic in Rochester is founded by the Mayo brothers.

1920 Prohibition begins on January 17 with the Eighteenth Amendment, or Volstead Act, named after Andrew Volstead of Minnesota.

1968 The American Indian Movement begins in Minnesota.

1978 Minnesota's supreme court orders the Reserve Mining Company to control its pollution of Lake Superior.

1992 Mall of America opens.

1999 Former professional wrestler Jesse Ventura is elected governor.

Fast Facts

Minnesota state capitol

Statehood date	May 11, 1858, the 32nd state
Origin of state name	From the Dakota words for water—*minne*—and cloudy or sky-tinted—*sotah*
State capital	St. Paul
State nickname	North Star State, Gopher State, Land of 10,000 Lakes
State motto	*L'Etoile du Nord* (The Star of the North)
State bird	Loon
State flower	Pink and white lady's slipper
State fish	Walleye
State gem	Lake Superior agate
State song	"Hail! Minnesota"
State tree	Norway (or red) pine
State fair	Late August to early September in St. Paul

Loon

Lake Superior

Total area; rank	86,943 sq. mi. (225,182 sq km); 12th
Land; rank	79,617 sq. mi. (206,208 sq km); 14th
Water; rank	7,326 sq. mi. (18,974 sq km); 4th
Inland water; **rank**	4,780 sq. mi. (12,380 sq km); 3rd
Great Lakes water; **rank**	2,546 sq. mi. (6,594 sq km); 5th
Geographic center	Crow Wing, 10 miles (16 km) southwest of Brainerd
Latitude and longitude	Minnesota is located approximately between 43° 30' and 49° 23' N and 89° 29' and 97° 13' W
Highest point	Eagle Mountain, 2,301 feet (702 m)
Lowest point	Lake Superior, 602 feet (184 m)
Largest city	Minneapolis
Number of counties	87
Population; rank	4,387,029 (1990 census); 20th
Density	52 persons per sq. mi. (20 per sq km)
Population distribution	70% urban, 30% rural

Burntside Lake

Ethnic distribution (does not equal 100%)	
White	94.41%
African-American	2.17%
Asian and Pacific Islanders	1.78%
Hispanic	1.23%
Native American	1.14%
Other	0.50%

Record high temperature	114°F (46°C) at Beardsley on July 29, 1917, and at Moorhead on July 6, 1936

Record low temperature	−60°F (−51°C) at Tower on February 2, 1996
Average July temperature	70°F (21°C)
Average January temperature	8°F (−13°C)
Average annual precipitation	26 inches (66 cm)

Superior National Forest

Natural Areas and Historic Sites

National Monuments

Grand Portage is the site of a major eighteenth-century fur-trading center. Visitors can see a canoe house, rebuilt great hall, and Grand Portage.

Pipestone offers tourists a chance to see pipestone quarries and tall-grass prairies on 283 acres (115 ha) of scenic Minnesota land.

National Parks

Voyageurs, near International Falls, was formed by glaciers. Its varied landscape includes beaver ponds, islands, and swamps.

National River and Recreation Areas

Mississippi provides visitors with views of the beginning of the longest river in the United States, as well as recreational areas along the river.

National Scenic Riverways

St. Croix is 252 miles (405 km) long and was one of the first riverways designated as Wild and Scenic by the National Park Service.

State Parks

Minnesota has sixty-eight state parks, all designed to preserve the state's landscape. In Charles A. Lindbergh State Park, visitors picnic

Randall Cunningham

close to a stone watertower with the Charles Lindbergh Sr. home across from the park. Fort Snelling State Park in the Twin Cities provides opportunities for biking and hiking along the Mississippi and Minnesota Rivers, as well as a chance to see old Fort Snelling.

Sports Teams

NCAA Teams (Division 1)
University of Minnesota Golden Gophers

Major League Baseball
Minnesota Twins

National Basketball Association
Minnesota Timberwolves

National Football League
Minnesota Vikings

National Hockey League
Minnesota Wild

Women's National Basketball Association
Minnesota Lynx

Minneapolis Institute of Arts

Cultural Institutions

Libraries
The *Minnesota Historical Society Library and Collections* offers visitors a history of the state through a photograph collection that dates back to 1850.

The *Minnesota Indian Women's Resource Center* library in Minneapolis provides information relating to American Indian women, including parenting, local Native American history, and chemical dependency.

University of St. Thomas

At the *Minnesota Valley Regional Library* in Mankato, children enjoy the reading room dedicated to author Maud Hart Lovelace, who is a native of Mankato.

Museums

The *Minneapolis Institute of Arts* houses 85,000 pieces of art and has collections ranging from ancient textiles to modern American art.

The *Saint Louis County Heritage and Arts Center*, also known as the Duluth Depot, is a renovated train station that houses several art galleries and museums.

The *Science Museum of Minnesota* in St. Paul has existed since 1907 and has a giant-screened Omni theater, numerous exhibits, and special events related to science.

The *Walker Art Center* in Minneapolis has a world-renowned art museum, sculpture garden, and theater for performing arts.

Performing Arts

Minnesota has two major symphony orchestras, two major dance companies, and two professional theater companies.

Universities and Colleges

In the mid-1990s, Minnesota had sixty-two public and forty-four private institutions of higher learning.

Annual Events

January–March

Grand Vinterslass Fest in Grand Rapids (January)

Ice Box Days winter festival in International Falls (January)

John Beargrease Sled Dog Race between Duluth and Grand Marais (January)

St. Paul Winter Carnival (late January–early February)

Duluth Winter Sports Festival (January–February)

The Children's Museum

Scottish Country Fair

International Eelpout Festival in Walker (February)

Minnesota Finlandia Ski Marathon in Bemidji (February)

April–June

Festival of Nations in St. Paul (April or May)

Swayed Pines Folk Fest in Collegeville (April)

Cinco de Mayo in St. Paul (May)

Scottish Country Fair in St. Paul (May)

Grandma's Marathon in Duluth (June)

Rochesterfest in Rochester (June)

July–September

Art in the Park in Albert Lea (July)

Heritagefest in New Ulm (July)

Taste of Minnesota food festival in St. Paul (July)

Wheels, Wings & Water Festival in St. Cloud (July)

Minneapolis Aquatennial (July)

Automobile racing at the Brainerd International Raceway (July–August)

Bayfront Blues Festival in Duluth (August)

Country Music Festival in Detroit Lakes (August)

Ethnic Days in Chisholm (August)

Fishermen's Picnic in Grand Marais (August)

Renaissance Fair in Shakopee (August–September)

Minnesota State Fair in St. Paul (August–September)

Dakota Public Powwow in Mankato (September)

Dozinky: A Czechoslovakian Harvest Festival in New Prague (September)

Western Minnesota Steam Threshers Reunion in Rollag (September)

Robert Bly

October–December

Halloween Festival in Anoka (October)

Oktoberfest in New Ulm (October)

Holidazzle Parade in Minneapolis (December)

Folkways of Christmas in Shakopee (December)

Christmas in the Village in Montevideo (December)

New Year's Eve Family Events in Minneapolis (December)

Famous People

Harry Andrew Blackmun (1908–1999)	Supreme Court justice
Robert Elwood Bly (1926–)	Poet
Warren Earl Burger (1907–1995)	Supreme Court chief justice
William Orville Douglas (1898–1980)	Supreme Court justice
Bob Dylan (1941–)	Singer and songwriter
F. Scott Fitzgerald (1896–1940)	Author
James Earle Fraser (1876–1953)	Sculptor
Judy Garland (1922–1969)	Actor and singer
Jean Paul Getty (1892–1976)	Businessman
Daniel Greysolon, Sieur du Lhut (1636–1710)	Explorer
Hubert H. Humphrey (1911–1978)	Vice president
Garrison Keillor (1942–)	Radio host and humorist
Elizabeth Kenny, or Sister Kenny (1880–1952)	Nurse
Jessica Lange (1949–)	Actor
Sinclair Lewis (1885–1951)	Author
Little Crow (1820?–1863)	Dakota Indian chief

F. Scott Fitzgerald

Roger Maris (1934–1985)	Professional baseball player
Charles Horace Mayo (1865–1939)	Physician
William James Mayo (1861–1939)	Physician
Walter Mondale (1928–)	Vice president
Zebulon Pike (1779–1813)	Army officer and explorer
Alexander Ramsey (1815–1903)	Politician
Jane Russell (1921–)	Actor
Charles M. Schultz (1922–)	Cartoonist
Harold Edward Stassen (1907–)	Public official
DeWitt Wallace (1889–1981)	Editor and publisher
Laura Ingalls Wilder (1867–1957)	Author
David Mark (Dave) Winfield (1951–)	Professional baseball player

Bob Dylan

To Find Out More

History

- Carlson, Jeffrey. *A Historical Album of Minnesota*. Brookfield, CT: Millbrook, 1993.

- Fradin, Dennis Brindell. *Minnesota.* Danbury, CT: Children's Press, 1997.

- King, Sandra, Michael Dorris, and Catherine Whipple (photographer). *Shannon: An Ojibway Dancer*. Minneapolis, MN: First Avenue Editions, 1993.

- O'Hara, Megan, and Tim Rummelhoff (illustrator). *Pioneer Farm: Living on a Farm in the 1800's*. Mankato, MN: Blue Earth Books, 1998.

- Thompson, Kathleen. *Minnesota*. Austin, TX: Raintree/Steck Vaughn, 1996.

Biography

- Davis, Lucille. *The Mayo Brothers: Doctors to the World*. Danbury, CT: Children's Press, 1998.

- Giblin, James Cross. *Charles A. Lindbergh: A Human Hero*. New York: Clarion Books, 1997.

- Paulsen, Gary. *Father Water, Mother Woods*. New York: Delacorte, 1994.

Fiction

- Paulsen, Gary. *Popcorn Days and Buttermilk Nights*. New York: Viking Press, 1989.

- Wilder, Laura Ingalls. *On the Banks of Plum Creek*. New York: HarperTrophy, 1973.

Websites

- **Minnesota Department of Natural Resources**
  http://www.dnr.state.mn.us
  A guide to Minnesota's parks and forests

- **Minnesota State Government**
  http://www.state.mn.us
  Tracks current state legislation, offers an archive of state of the state addresses, and gives general information about Minnesota's government.

- **University of Minnesota**
  http://www.umn.edu
  Provides information about all aspects of Minnesota's college system.

Addresses

- **International Wolf Center**
  1396 Highway 169
  Ely, MN 55731-8129
  For information about wolves and the environment

- **Minnesota Historical Society**
  345 Kellogg Boulevard West
  St. Paul, MN 55102-1906
  For information about Minnesota history

- **Minnesota Office of Tourism**
  Travel Information Center
  500 Metro Square
  121 Seventh Place
  St. Paul, MN 55101-2146
  For information about travel and recreation in Minnesota

- **Office of the Governor**
  130 State Capitol
  75 Constitution Avenue
  St. Paul, MN 55155
  For general information about Minnesota

Index

Page numbers in *italics* indicate illustrations.

Meet the Author

When Martin Hintz was a young man, some of his best summers were spent visiting relatives in Minneapolis. He fished in the city's nearby lakes, visited Dayton's department store, and watched Fourth of July fireworks in the city skies.

When the time came for college, Hintz returned to Minnesota. He graduated with a journalism degree from the College of St. Thomas. Vice president and Minnesotan Hubert H. Humphrey spoke at his college commencement. For fun, during Hintz's years as a student in the Twin Cities, he and his friends built rafts to ride the Mississippi, visited jazz clubs and theaters, played soccer with students from other area universities, hiked park trails, and enjoyed the St. Paul Winter Carnival.

A journalist, Martin Hintz has written two guidebooks and dozens of magazine and newspaper articles about Minnesota as well as a book about the port of Duluth. He is also the author of several books in the Enchantment of the World and America the Beautiful series, published by Children's Press.

To write this book, Hintz did library and Internet research and conducted interviews with Minnesotans. He augmented it with his extensive firsthand knowledge of the state.

Martin Hintz lives in River Hills, Wisconsin, with his wife, Pam Percy, a producer for Wisconsin Public Radio.

Photo Credits

Photographs ©:

AllSport USA: 7 bottom, 123, 131 top (Matthew Stockman)

Archive Photos: 46 (Bernard Gotfryd), 40 (Potter Collection), 23, 24, 44, 47, 61 top, 71 top, 120

Brown Brothers: 19, 34 bottom, 37, 39

Corbis-Bettmann: 78 (AFP), 115 (Philip Gould), 33 top, 42, 81, 87, 119 (UPI)

Envision: 91 (Peter Johansky)

Greg Ryan/Sally Beyer: back cover, 2, 6 top right, 6 top left, 7 top center, 14, 25, 33 bottom, 50, 51, 52, 57, 61 bottom, 62, 63, 64, 68, 72, 74, 89, 101, 103, 110, 111, 129 bottom, 132 top, 133

Liaison Agency, Inc.: 113, 134 top (Millicent Harvey), 109 (Eric Sander), 8 (Glenn Short), 92 (Aaron A. Strong), 117, 135 (Anthony Suau)

Martin Hintz: 88

Minnesota Historical Society: 82 (Golling), 36, 38, 95

Minnesota Office of Tourism: 6 bottom, 7 top right, 11, 16, 67, 69, 73, 75, 84, 98, 104, 106, 112, 121, 124, 128 bottom, 131 bottom, 132 bottom

National Geographic Image Collection: 107 (Joel Sartore);

North Wind Picture Archives: 15, 17, 18, 28, 29, 30, 34 top, 94

Photo Researchers: 65 (Tom & Pat Leeson)

Photofest: 118

Star Tribune/Minneapolis, St. Paul: 86

Stock Montage, Inc.: 22 (The Newberry Library), 20, 35

Superstock, Inc.: 114, 134 bottom

The Image Works: 54, 99 (M. Douglas), 102 (M. Everton), 48 (Mark Godfrey), 6 top center, 13 (M. Siluk)

Tony Stone Images: 60 (Cathlyn Melloan), 76, 77, 128 top (Peter Pearson), cover, 7 top left, 9, 53, 66, 130 (Ryan/Beyer)

Visuals Unlimited: 56 (Bill Banaszewski), 71 bottom (Louie Bunde), 108 (D. Long), 59, 129 top (Roger A. Powell)

Maps by XNR Productions, Inc.